Unsolicited Praise for *No Time for Goodbyes*

"What a book! What comfort! What insight! This book must be made available in all countries."
— *Joan Isherwood, children killed, Cheshire, England*

"This is one of the best grief books I've read – and I've read them all!"
— *Laurette Hupman, publishing consultant, Wilmette, Illinois*

"This book should be in the hands of every victim of homicide. To my knowledge, there is no other resource that so touches this unique group of people."
— *Rhonda Anthony, MADD, Fresno, California*

"As a bereavement facilitator, I've read a lot about grief and related topics. When I read the dedication page in your book, I thought it might be different, and I wasn't disappointed. A spiritual warmth emits from its pages that is healing. I highly recommend it."
— *Mary Hammericksen, Seattle, Washington*

Thank you so much for your sensitive writing of *No Time for Goodbyes*. I wish you the very best in your future endeavors.
— *Joseph Biden, U.S. Senator from Delaware*

"For fifteen months, your book stayed in my purse. Now I keep it by my bed. Thanks so much, Janice. Although I've never met you, you are the one who gave me strength to go on."
— *Cindi Winkle, fiancé killed, Aumsville, Oregon*

"I lost all my family within three years, and grief overwhelmed me. Thank you so much for your book, which was sent by a friend. I wish you all the best for your important work."
— *Dr. Ruthmarijke Smeding, The Netherlands*

"This book is invaluable for hospice counselors and for families grieving a violent death. It adds priceless emotional and practical information about grief. *No Time for Goodbyes* is rich with personal testament to the love and courage of survivors."
— *Joyce Dace-Lombard, grief counselor, Camarillo, California*

"You have put together a knowledgeable, compassionate, and factual book to help those of us who have been suddenly thrust into the unwilling role of victims. God bless you for your insight and wisdom. I thank you from the bottom of my heart for this lifeline."

– Patricia O'Connor, child killed, Jackson, New Jersey

"*No Time for Goodbyes* will become one of the books I most highly recommend to any surviving family member. I never thought I would curl up with a good book and spend most of the time crying."

– Donna Lamonaco, law enforcement husband killed, Brandywine, New Jersey

"There is sound advice here, not only for those grieving a violent death, but for those who want to comfort them."

– Review, Sydney Morning Herald, Sydney, Australia

"I want to thank you for putting into words the heartbreak and utter devastation one feels when a loved one has been suddenly taken from you."

– Gloria Cook, child killed, Gibsonia, Pennsylvania

"Janice Lord provides excellent practical suggestions for coming to grips with grief and coping with the specific problems encountered."

– Review, American Trauma Society

"As part of our counseling program, we have discovered that *No Time for Goodbyes* is very helpful in giving families tools to reach some resolution of their loss."

– Judy Batchelor, grief counselor, Detroit, Michigan

"Why didn't I find your book two years ago? It seems like eternity since I journeyed to that black pit of emotions within. Your words helped me realize how far I've come. At times when I feel the shadow of that time, I pick up your book and realize that I am not alone."

– Sue Look, friend killed, South Perth, Australia

"I couldn't make sense of this world any longer after my sister and her daughter were murdered. Your book helped me a great deal. Thank you for writing it."

– Sandra Mulcah, St. Paul, Minnesota

"Your book is terrific! You're right on target about tragic death."

– Lauri Ware, funeral director, Fort Worth, Texas

NO TIME FOR GOODBYES

Coping With Sorrow, Anger, and Injustice
After a Tragic Death

By
Janice Harris Lord

Compassion Press
A division of Compassion Books, Inc.
Burnsville, North Carolina

NO TIME FOR GOODBYES

Published by:
Compassion Press
A division of Compassion Books, Inc.
7036 State Highway 80 South
Burnsville, NC 28714
828-675-5909

Copyright 1987, 1988, 1990, 1991, 2000,
and 2006 by Janice Harris Lord
First printing 1987
Second Edition January 1988 Revised
Third printing 1989
Third Edition 1990 Revised
Fifth Printing 1990
Fourth Edition 1991 Revised
Seventh Printing 1992
Eight Printing 1993
Ninth Printing 1994
Tenth Printing 1995
Eleventh Printing 1996
Twelfth Printing 1997
Thirteenth Printing 1997
Fourteenth Printing 1999
Fifth Edition Printing 2000
Sixteenth Printing 2001
Seventeenth Printing 2001
Eighteenth Printing 2002
Sixth Edition 2006 Revised

Library of Congress Control Number: 2006926916

ISBN-13: 978-1-878321-30-5
ISBN-10: 1-878321-30-7
1.Bereavement - psychological aspects. 2. Violent
deaths - psychological aspects. 3. Grief. I Title

DEDICATION

To the countless victims of violence who
dared to open their hearts to me
and thereby carved into my heart
a deepened capacity to care.

I can never fully understand your pain,
but I treasure your willingness to allow
me to stand with you
in your suffering.

ACKNOWLEDGEMENTS

Many people planted seeds throughout the years that blossomed into the 6th edition of this book. So many colleagues contributed to its evolution that it would be difficult to mention each by name. Most important, however, it has been the victims who shared their stories with me who breathed life into these pages. I remember with gratitude each one who is quoted, and acknowledge the lessons I learned from those who are not.

A major note of gratitude goes to *Dr. Dennis Saleeby*, my graduate social work professor, who required readings about death and dying before it became popular. It was in his class that I developed my first workshop on the subject, and I continue to hold him in high regard for his focus on strength-based social work.

Mothers Against Drunk Driving (MADD) first made the book possible by allowing me time to write while I served in the position of National Director of Victim Services. The national staff, board of directors, and chapters of MADD have been more than supportive of my work for nearly 25 years.

I am deeply indebted to *Dr. Robert Weiss* of the Work and Family Research Unit at the University of Massachusetts. Dr. Weiss believed that my papers and brochures would be beneficial to families in which a loved one had been killed. Through his inspired paper, *Will it Always Feel This Way? For the Parent Whose Child has been Killed*, he confirmed my belief that it is respectable to write from the heart as well as the head.

I am grateful to *Dr. Hannelore Wass, Dr. Camille Wortman, Dr. Darrin Lehman, Dr. Therese Rando,* and *Dr. Ted Rynearson* for their excellent research and publications that formed an invaluable cornerstone for my work with victims. I especially thank them for reviewing the book during their busy schedules.

I thank attorney and former judge *Cathy Stayman Evans* for her diligent review of the chapter on criminal justice. Civil attorneys *William Shernoff, Charles Lipcon, and Doug Roberts*, as well as *Fred Beck, Bob Plunk,* and the late *Ralph Jackson* all deserve appreciation for their consultation regarding financial recovery for victims. Attorneys *David Flowers* and *Jim Reynolds* were especially helpful, as was financial planner, *Jerry Cosby*.

While a multitude of victims were remembered and quoted in the book, special thanks go to *Janet Barton, Greg Novak, Bob* and *Pat Preston, Ralph Shelton, Howard Velzy*, and the late *Betty Jane Spencer* for reading the manuscript and offering constructive criticism.

The second edition was greatly enhanced by the addition of the chapter on suicide. For that, I am grateful for the encouragement of *Anne Seymour*.

With the assistance of *Stephanie Frogge*, additions were made to the Death of a Brother or Sister chapter in the fourth edition.

The fifth edition added new findings from the emerging field of trauma grief, an enhanced chapter on Spirituality, and a new chapter on Death of a Significant Other, Friend, or Colleague. I thank my friend and colleague, *Catherine Madigan*, for her sensitivity as a victim advocate and exquisite editing skills as a journalist in helping me revise the fifth edition.

After more than a year of the book's unavailability, I thank my colleagues for their patience in awaiting this new, totally enhanced and revised sixth edition. *Bruce Greene*, of my new publishing house, *Compassion Books, Inc.*, is also to be commended for his patience and gentle support throughout this transition process. We long ago passed the 100,000 mark in sales of the book, and although the information in early editions remains timeless, the field of trauma death continues to expand, allowing for new knowledge to be added with each edition. We publish this new edition with the hope that it will touch the hearts and minds of those who need it. May their grieving and growing be a fitting memorial to the spirits of those they have loved.

Janice Harris Lord
June, 2006

CONTENTS

PREFACE

Before beginning my work with those whose loved ones had been killed suddenly, I thought I was accustomed to the aftermath of violence. I had worked with physically and sexually abused children. I had counseled battered women. I thought I had witnessed the pinnacle of rage, the depths of despair. I was naïve.

In 1983, as the first Director of Victim Services at the national headquarters of *Mothers Against Drunk Driving* (MADD), my perspective changed. During my first week of phone calls and letters from victims, I realized that grieving the loss of a loved one who had been killed suddenly, violently, and senselessly differs significantly from grief following an anticipated death. That's not to say that it's worse than witnessing someone you love slowly disintegrate toward death. It may not be worse, but it is different.

That first year, I met Mary Anna Downing a few days after her son, Eddie, was killed by a drunk driver. Just a little more than a year before, her son, Jimmy, had also been killed by a drunk driver. After Eddie's funeral, I watched his casket lowered into the ground beside his brother, whose grave was still fresh, without grass or tombstone. My mind spun in the awareness that Mary Anna Downing was now tasked with buying headstones for two children, negotiating with four insurance companies, and participating in two separate criminal procedures, each with its own myriad of players. A school cafeteria worker, Mary Anna supplemented her meager income by selling Avon products. She was now too devastated to return to work. I wondered how she would survive.

A few weeks later, I met Carl and Mary Mittag. Still grieving the loss of Mary's father to cancer, their family now faced the sudden death of Mary's mother, aunt, and cousin while vacationing in Florida. I witnessed their agony as they attempted to cope not only with their deep grief, but the painful death imagery in their minds. Companioning them over the years, we faced significant frustration brought about by the criminal justice system, complicated wrongful death civil suits, confusing insurance settlement proposals in states far from their home. The criminal trial resulted in a verdict of "not guilty" for the driver, although the evidence was clear that he had been intoxicated. Two years later, the wrongful death civil suits were still pending, and not one cent of insurance money had been paid to the family.

Later that first year, I met Betty Jane Spencer, and our relationship continued to grow until she died in 2005. Betty Jane's four sons were shot and killed execution-style in their rural Indiana home. Betty Jane was wounded, but survived. As she looked back on the events of that day, she said, "I was killed, too. I just didn't die."

Out of the ashes of her experience, however, Betty Jane kindled motivation to accomplish multiple legislative changes for victims' rights in Indiana. She eventually became a great source of compassionate strength for many other victims who leaned on her.

If you commented about her strength, though, Betty Jane would say, "No, I'm not strong, but I do have courage." She attributed her definition of courage to John Wayne: "Courage is being afraid and saddling up anyway." Betty Jane never stopped being afraid that the boys' killers would eventually get out of prison and return to kill her, too. The fear didn't stop her, however, from reaching out to others with a wisdom gained only through suffering.

I have facilitated support groups in which every member was grieving the death of someone they loved to a violent, senseless act. In these groups, I witnessed the wonderful healing power of a stranger, struggling with his own grief, to say, "I understand something of what you are going through. I'm walking in similar shoes."

I do not label myself a victim, even though my uncle killed himself while driving under the influence of drugs in the 1940's, long before it was considered a crime. I would never say that I "understand" what it is like to have a close loved one killed, even though my first-hand work with victims, ongoing education, and research over the years have helped me develop a cache of insight that I hope will help suddenly bereaved families.

While I have read and participated in many studies, this book is not a scholarly report on trauma grief research. Much of that research, however, guides my ever-evolving theoretical base for working with victims. While the book is written for bereaved families, I believe it can also heighten the awareness of professionals seeking to understand more about the homicide or suicide survivor experience. After all, those who have walked in the shoes are always our best teachers.

The book focuses on the needs of family members and friends when someone loved has been killed. It explores common survivor reactions to the trauma they have suffered. I hope it helps them realize that they are not alone and enables them to consider practical suggestions for coming to grips with their reactions and with the systems with which they will be forced to interact.

It is written to help those who fear that they can never heal, to realize that somehow, someday, with time and effort, they will actually begin to feel better. Total healing or recovery is not the goal. The reality of living in a potentially frightening world will remain. How each survivor chooses to carve out memories will differ. Some may choose to focus on the one who was killed and try to ignore their own suffering for a time. When they are ready to feel a little better, however, I believe their burden can be lightened somewhat by reading of the experiences of other similar pilgrims.

This book is written in the spirit of a man whose mother, father, wife, and brother were murdered in the Holocaust, but who was able to say:

"...Everything can be taken from a man but one thing:
the loss of the human freedoms to choose one's attitude
in any given set of circumstances..."
– *Viktor Frankl, Man's Search for Meaning*

Said a bit more simply by *Bertha Calloway,* founder of the Great Plains Black Museum:

"We cannot direct the wind, but we can adjust the sails."

Chapter One

YOUR GRIEF IS UNIQUE

Someone you love has been killed, perhaps in a vehicular crash or a freak accident, perhaps murdered. Maybe this person took his or her own life. Perhaps life was snuffed out in a military disaster or an act of terrorism. Pain too deep for words may be your experience. Even if you have begun your pilgrimage toward feeling better, that kind of pain may still be a vivid memory.

Death may not have been new to you when this death happened. During your lifetime, you may have lost family members or friends to terminal illnesses or old age. Death is rarely easy to accept. However, most human beings recover, and in time, memories of the good times replace memories of the sad final days.

This death is different.

The sudden, violent death that took your loved one probably feels unlike anything else you have experienced. Few, if any, family tragedies are as traumatic as the death of a loved one by homicide, suicide, or some terrible accident. You may be angrier that you have ever been and sadder than you thought possible. You may have frightening thoughts. You may do strange things. You may be afraid you are "going crazy."

Do not be alarmed. Few people experiencing traumatic grief "go crazy." Moving through your misery can feel so devastating, though, that you begin to question your own sanity.

Most people can accept the fact that "accidents" happen. But a sudden death has only a few similarities with an expected death. It feels even more traumatic if the death came both suddenly and violently. In criminal victimization, those left behind have a difficult time grasping the reality that another human being chose to be negligent or to select a victim to brutalize. It makes no sense at all.

You may feel alienated by family members or friends who seem to reject you because they don't understand why you are taking it so hard. They may not know that "being killed" differs from "dying." They may not realize that simply showing up and holding you means a lot more than words. Services or programs designed to help people cope with anticipated deaths may seem superficial to you.

Families can never be prepared for the violent or sudden death of a loved one. Nor are they prepared to face weeks, months, and even years of waiting until a criminal case is resolved and insurance claims and civil suits are settled. Individuals and institutions that are counted on for support sometimes fail. Unfortunately, many of those who attempt to help, including some professionals who should know better, don't understand that grieving after a traumatic death like homicide or suicide is intense and long-lasting for most people.

Each person grieves differently. Yet, while each person's reaction to what happened is unique, studies indicate that survivors who suffer similar losses often benefit from sharing each others' grief journeys.

How you grieve depends on a number of things:

• The way you learned to cope with stresses in your life before this tragedy;

• The quality of the relationship you had with the person who was killed;

• Your level of success in dealing with the criminal justice system, insurance companies, and the myriad of other systems you must face in the aftermath of your tragedy;

• Your religious beliefs and ethnic customs;

• Your personal resilience, or ability to re-establish equilibrium following distressing events;

• The amount of support your family and friends offer while you are grieving, and...

• Your physical and mental health.

It is amazing but true that a few people seem to handle trauma pretty well. They are able to return to a fulfilling life soon after their loved one dies. Most of these people are privileged to have strong support from their family and friends and a substantial supply of good memories about the one who died. Many of these people believe that their loved one lives on spiritually. However, most families in which someone has been killed have a very difficult time coping, even those who believe that their loved one's spirit continues to live.

Anticipated Death

Let us look for a moment at what we know about grief after an anticipated and non-violent death. This will help you understand some of your unique reactions to homicide or suicide. It is tempting to label anticipated and non-violent death as "normal," even though few people in grief, even in the best of circumstances, feel "normal." However, the griever who knows ahead of time that death is approaching may react differently from you.

When people learn that a loved one is likely to die, they may not believe it at first. They may seek several medical opinions to be sure it is really that bad, and rightly so.

As they begin to believe that death is, indeed, forthcoming, they may get angry. Perhaps they are angry that modern science can develop machines as miraculous as computers, but can't find a cure for their loved one's condition. They may be angry with God for allowing death. They may pray fervently for God to intervene, and then feel frustrated if God doesn't seem to answer their prayers.

They may be sad and depressed as they face the fact that their loved one will die. They may long for relief for their loved one as they see his or her body deteriorate.

When both the dying person and the family members come to accept the reality that death is imminent, they have an opportunity to express their feelings for one another, resolve problems, and relate lovingly and honestly during the last days.

Even in the best of circumstances, though, survivors are often surprised to find themselves going through many of the same reactions of disbelief, anger, and sadness after the death. It seems to be a part of human nature that emotionally healthy human beings resist death, their own as well as someone else's, and that is as it should be.

Approaching death can bring people closer together or it can cause them to distance themselves from each other. Either way, this preparation time is believed to cushion the impact of the death. Even though sad, many people feel relieved that the suffering is finally over.

Coming to grips with an anticipated death usually takes from three to twenty-four months, according to most research. Sometimes it takes longer. Most people find that if they "lean in" to grieving, allow their emotions to flow, and talk openly about their loss, they will, little by little, be cleansed of much of the pain. Active mourning helps grief. Those who attempt to deny their grief and pretend that nothing has happened may have more difficulty.

Traumatic Death

Your experience may be quite unlike that just described because death came to your loved one suddenly. You had no time to say "good-bye," or "I love you."

> "The sad part is that she died alone. There was no last 'I love you' or 'Thank you' or 'Hey, I really appreciate all you do.' There were no soft smiles, no caring words. Only screams. Screams that echoed through the empty chambers of my mind where laughter once reigned."
>
> *– Tammy Luke, whose friend,*
> *Laura Porter, was killed*

Violence of the Death

The death your loved one faced may have been violent. Perhaps his or her body was mutilated by a gunshot or a knife wound. Perhaps it was a vehicular crash caused by someone who chose to drive too fast or while intoxicated. Witnessing the results of a violent death can be extremely painful.

It may be important for you to know that when people are seriously injured, they often undergo shock and do not immediately experience pain. The brain produces chemicals that numb both physical and emotional responses. Many who have recovered from serious injury say it was some time before they felt pain, even if they drifted in and out of consciousness. Most do not remember the point of impact, whether from an automobile crash, gunshot, or other form of trauma.

Therefore, your shock upon learning of the tragedy may actually have been more terrifying that the experience of the person who died. Even so, you may be thinking that you would have done anything to prevent your loved one's body from being violated that way.

Human beings have personalities, and most people believe they also have spirits or souls. But bodies are also important. You grieve the loss of your loved one's personality and spirit, but you also grieve the loss of his or her living body. You saw it. You touched it. It touched you. You miss it. That loss is very biological in nature and can cause people to react primitively.

To My Dead Daughter

Fair daughter, sister, friend and heart-mate;
Soul's child, Eros, muse and mirror.
I kiss the arching feet,
the small cold hands, the purpled lids.
A drop of blood from your smooth brow
I lick, like a mother beast,
mewing, nuzzling, howling
over its cub.
Mad with pain.
I stroke your body, heavy now,
that had such lightness, grace,
its gold warmth now yellowing.

No. This is not you!
You are not here.
I search, my darling, everywhere.
My stunned feet grope forest paths.
Through shared waters my body moves.
I float upon your river of dark hair.
Are you there?
I grasp the air.
                    — *Anita Huffington,*
                        whose daughter was killed

You not only miss the living presence and body of your loved one, but you may feel guilty because you were unable to protect your loved one, even if you know that what happened was not your fault.

Because of the condition of your loved one's body, you may not have been able to view it at the hospital or funeral home. If this was the case, you now rely on fantasy to form a picture of how you think he or she looked. Many people discover that the death images they developed in their minds were worse than what actually happened, when they later view investigation photos or photos that may have been taken at the medical examiner's office or funeral home. Perhaps you chose not to view the body, or maybe someone told you that you could not. Your ethnic or spiritual beliefs may prohibit viewing. Many faith groups do not view deceased bodies, other than a few people who prepare the body for burial. Within Christianity and a few other faiths, viewing is accepted and even encouraged. Regardless of the reason, if you did not view, you may still have some lingering doubt that your loved one actually died. You may find yourself expecting him or her to walk through the door or call on the telephone at any minute. Most survivors feel this way for awhile, but it may be more likely if you did not see your loved one's body after the death.

Most people who chose to and were allowed to view their loved one are glad they did. If you wanted to look or touch but were unable to, you may have to find other ways to assure yourself of the reality of the death.

> "Michael was so badly battered, with many head injuries. I refused to let his three younger brothers go into the hospital room. I regret that now. In an effort to spare them, I robbed them of their last chance to see their brother alive. Even though the casket was closed to the public, our family did get to see and touch his body before the funeral. His brother James, 15, slipped Mike's graduation key and tassel in his breast pocket before we closed the casket."
>
> *– Rita Chiavacci, whose son*
> *Michael, age 19, was killed*

Funeral directors generally allow family members as much choice as possible about viewing the body of their loved one. Most people know what they want to do. If the funeral director describes the condition of the body, family members usually make the right choice about viewing. Not everyone in the family may make the same choice, and each person's choice should be honored.

Funeral directors also are encouraged to take photos of the deceased in their final state. Family members who choose not to view the body immediately may wish to look at photographs weeks, month, or years later.

Other options are possible for those who did not have an opportunity to see the body. Law enforcement, fire department, medical examiner, and the prosecutor's office investigators usually have photos. The photos, however, can be stark and graphic because they are not retouched like studio photos. These agencies, understanding themselves to be compassionate, may be reluctant to allow family members to view photographs. You may need to be assertive in your request, if it is important to you. Understand, too, that you will not be able to view photos that may be used as evidence until the justice proceedings are finished.

The organization, *Parents of Murdered Children*, recommends the following procedure for viewing pictures of the deceased: The person wishing to view the photos is encouraged to take their closest support person with them to the agency that will allow them to view the pictures. The person in custody of the photographs is asked to place each picture in a separate envelope, arranging them in order with the least offensive or violent photo on top and the most disturbing photo on bottom. The support person is shown the first photograph, and then is asked to describe it to the primary family member or friend. This gives the primary viewer two sources of information: the description of the photo from the support person and their observation of how the support person reacts to the photo. On that basis, the primary viewer can make a reasonably informed decision about whether to look at the photograph.

Many times, only one or two photos are viewed, but the family member may choose to take copies of the other photos home to view later. If the criminal justice case is complete and there is no longer a legal need for securing the photos within the agency, the family should have that right to view the photos.

Viewing bodies at the scene of the crime is a similar issue. Once emergency medical care has been administered, and the crime scene has been properly recorded by the law enforcement agency, survivors should be allowed a choice about seeing, touching, or holding the body of their loved one. Attendants should be very clear in describing the condition of the body so the survivor's choice is an informed one. Again, most people know what they want to do once they know what they will see.

Very rarely does a survivor report regret after being allowed to view or touch their loved one's body. Most are grateful for the opportunity.

Many hospitals now allow family members to be present and touch their loved one through the dying experience, to witness life-saving measures, and to remain with the body as long as they wish if their loved one dies.

In some cases, a loved one discovers the body at the scene of the death. Family members frequently are the first to discover victims of murder or suicide. Vehicular crashes sometimes are witnessed by family or friends. Shock, numbness, and rage are natural reactions at a violent death scene because of no time for psychological preparation. The visual and auditory imprint of a traumatic death scene can be overwhelming and long lasting because brain chemistry alterations, when in shock, can create indelible memories.

Professional counselors with expertise in trauma imagery can help those who are fixated on the death scene. This is accomplished through emotional support as the experience is described and specific techniques are used to help recall the memory with less horror. With help, positive memories of the loved one will replace distressing images. These techniques are generally more helpful with single-incident traumas than ongoing traumatic experiences such as family violence.

Untimeliness of the Death

A sudden death is never timely. Whether the one killed was your child, mate, parent, brother, sister, friend, or elderly parent or grandparent, the shock can feel devastating. Death is always sad, but having no time to psychologically prepare usually results in a more complicated mourning process.

Your Child

If your child was killed, a part of you may feel aborted, too. Your parental drive to nurture and protect remains, but it now has nowhere to go. A child's death feels terribly wrong. You expected to die before your child. It doesn't seem right that this natural pattern was reversed. This is true whether the one killed was a young child or an adult child. Your child is always your child.

> "No! You're lying,
> It can't be!" I screamed,
> as I ran about pounding my head.
> "I'm sorry," the officer replied,
> "but your son didn't make it.
> He's dead."
> "Oh, dear God, how can it be?"
> I cried.
> "He was just a kid of seventeen!"
> – *Florence (Mickey) Mikalauskas,*
> *whose son was killed*

Your Mate

If your mate was killed, you may have suddenly lost your best friend, lover, co-parent, financial partner, and primary confidant. Being forced to make major decisions alone, to maintain the family, and to grieve, all at the same time, can feel like a greater burden than you can carry.

"At 7:30 am, my wife died with me at her side. I never saw her conscious. I have nightmares about that moment even still. I feel I let her down. I wish I could have just looked into her eyes once and said, 'I love you.'

Our second Christmas without Michelle is now approaching. There are no words to explain the grief that I and our three children, Erika, 7, Kimberly, 5, and Jeffrey, 2, have gone through this past year. The two girls still have nightmares. Jeffrey never knew his mother. How can I explain a broken heart and broken dreams?"

– Joseph Lawrence,
whose 35-year-old wife was killed

Your Parent

If your parent was killed, no matter how old he or she was, you deeply regret that the death was so undignified. Many people say, "He lived a good, full life," but you may feel guilty about never having said, "Thank you for giving me life," or "Goodbye," or "I'm so sorry that your death came this way."

"February 12 was a very long day, the longest. My mother's surprise visit turned into tragedy. Now two days later, eyes red, I'm sitting on an airplane flying my mother's body home. How do you say to your brothers, 'Mom is dead, killed in a needless crash?'

I had had a rough year and, as always, Mom was coming to comfort me. Now, this is Mom's last flight home to Iowa. It was so quick, so unnecessary. I miss her so much I can hardly bear it."

– Barbara Brodt

Your Sibling

If your brother or sister was killed, you may find yourself feeling guilty about simply being alive, even though you know it is irrational. Siblings share so much history and have a great deal in common. A sibling's death can remind you of your own mortality. If your brother or sister could die in an instant, so can you. The pain swirling through families as they try to cope can make you feel like the wrong child died.

"Dale, I'm just so glad for the time we had together. And I'm glad we were close. But I'm so sad and so sorry we won't have any more laughter or good times together. I will always love you and I will never, ever stop missing you. I just pray that no other brother or sister will have to feel the way I feel now. There is an empty space inside of me that can't be filled again. No one can take your place."

– Debra Mumblo,
whose brother was killed

Your Friend or Colleague

If your friend or colleague was killed, you may feel like your own brother or sister is now gone. In this fast-paced, mobile society, relatives may be geographically remote or emotionally distant. Friends and colleagues can feel closer than family. If you worked together, you probably talked with your colleague nearly every day, more often than you visited with most of your relatives.

"That my wonderful young friend could be gunned down in an instant shattered me. I knew I had to open my arms to his family, but at the same time, I desperately needed people to see me as a legitimate mourner, too."

– Kimberly Rowland, whose friend
was murdered with a gun

Senselessness of the Death

Another difficult component of grieving the death of your loved one is the senselessness of the homicidal, suicidal, or negligent act itself. You can understand that bodies wear out with age or that cures for some diseases have not yet been discovered. However, most violent deaths are intentional or the result of negligence. Someone was at fault.

Murder is the brutal, purposeful assault of an unwilling victim. Suicide differs only in that the victim willed to die. Even though military families know the risk involved in combat, most expect their loved one to return home.

In an effort to make sense of the senseless, you search for blame. Many criminal offenders were previously incarcerated or institutionalized. If they had remained there, you believe this death might have been avoided. You cannot understand why the justice system failed to protect your loved one from this killer.

Most vehicular crashes result from someone's choice to be irresponsible. About half are caused by drunk drivers. Most involve speeding. Many are caused by people who refuse to stop and rest, and then fall asleep behind the wheel. Recent research shows that prescription sleeping pills are in the blood of many impaired drivers. Few crashes are truly accidental. Most could have been prevented.

One of the most difficult and complicated losses for families is a murder in which the offender was known: the baby-sitter who kills a child, the teenager who kills his date, the jealous lover who kills the "ex," the drunk driver who kills one of his own family members.

If you know the offender, your mind may be in turmoil with confusing and conflicting reactions. You may feel guilty because you did not choose to intervene sooner. It is difficult to blame someone you know. You may worry about what will happen to the offender in the criminal and civil justice systems. Knowing that your loved one's death could have been prevented may be one of the most difficult aspects of your grieving.

Criminal Justice Frustrations

Most violent deaths require involvement of the family with the criminal justice system. The required complex procedures can be difficult and frustrating. You may not understand why the State requires an autopsy. An autopsy is performed to determine the exact cause of death, which becomes a key component of the criminal trial. Autopsies are not always required after a suicide, but if the investigation reveals any questions about intent, an autopsy may be ordered to rule out homicide as the cause of death. You may be left out of meetings and hearings that you believe you should have a right to attend. Unless you are assertive, you may not be involved in decisions at critical stages of the criminal case. See Chapter 12, The Criminal Justice System, to learn how to become an active player in this process.

> "I contacted the District Attorney's office about two months after my children were killed. I was given the impression that my presence and questions were an imposition to the Assistant DA handling the case. To me, my children were human beings, not just reports lying on someone's desk. Was it wrong for me to want to see that the man who had killed my children was prosecuted?
>
> I was not told when the trial would be held and found

out only when it appeared in the newspaper. I wasn't allowed to be in the courtroom because my 'presence' might bias the jury. Yet the offender was present through the entire trial. The jury never saw pictures of my beautiful children and they never knew who I was as I sat alone in the hall the three days of the trial."
– Mary Mitchell, whose children, Bart, 5,
and Gayla, 7, were killed

Financial Stress

Your financial security may be threatened after the death of a loved one. Emergency medical care and funerals are costly. You may have missed several days or weeks of work. You may have difficulty concentrating when you return to work. Your limited productivity may threaten your job security, or you may have even lost your job. You may have paid for the travel of relatives to come to the funeral. All of that takes money. Chapter 13, Financial Issues, offers many practical suggestions for obtaining death-related financial assistance.

Spiritual Issues

Even if you never thought much about "life," "death," or "God" before, you may be thinking about these things now. On the other hand, you may have thought a lot about spiritual matters and devoted yourself to religious practices that gave you a sense of emotional and spiritual security. Now, your previous beliefs and practices may seem inadequate. This sense of alienation can cause you despair. It will take time and effort to reconstruct your beliefs and spiritual practices to accommodate this tragedy. You may refer to Chapter 10, Spirituality, to further explore this aspect of your experience.

Summary

I have not painted a pretty picture of the aftermath of sudden death. You knew your experience was far from "pretty" when you opened this book. Your loss was unanticipated. It was violent. It was unnecessary. It was untimely. It may have plunged you into a criminal justice system that is complex. You may suddenly find yourself under financial stress. And, you may be struggling to reconfigure a faith or philosophy that can sustain you.

It is not the purpose of this book to bewilder you or perplex you. Its purpose is to help you understand why your grief reaction is not like others you have experienced. It is to help you understand why you feel angry when others tell you that you should "get on with your life."

Don't be alarmed if you cry while reading this book. That only means that you need to cry. Grief and mourning usually include crying. It is painful, but it is healthy. Most people feel some relief after crying because it helps them get in touch with parts of themselves they couldn't touch in any other way. Crying also has been shown to remove toxins that the body stores up when it is highly stressed. The chemical composition of tears shed in grief differs significantly from that of tears shed while, for example, chopping an onion. Human beings have the capacity to cry for very good reasons.

Understanding more about the unique aspects of your traumatic grief will not change how you feel about your loved one, but it should enable you to feel more comfortable with yourself. It may enable you, also, to take what others say with a grain of salt if their expectations do not fit your own experience.

What I Want to Remember From This Chapter

Chapter Two

GRIEF AND MOURNING
FOLLOWING TRAUMA

We are all vulnerable to deep emotional reactions after a traumatic experience. These reactions are natural responses to an abnormal event. In other words, it is good to feel bad. Emotionally healthy human beings should not feel "normal" or "OK" when terrible things happen.

It is very important, however, for you to remember your strengths before this tragedy happened. The kind of person you were before will, to a large degree, determine how you react now and how soon you begin to feel better. If you are physically and emotionally healthy, if you had a good relationship with your loved one, if you have a supportive network of friends, if you feel basically in control of your life, and if you tend to view a crisis as a challenge rather than a catastrophe, you may begin to feel better more quickly than those who are not so fortunate.

No matter how "together" you are, however, beginning to heal from a traumatic and unexpected death requires patience and work. You will never be exactly the same again, but you will be much better than you may be now. Getting better means being able to:

- solve problems and complete tasks in your daily routine again,

- sleep well and have energy again,

- feel good enough about yourself to be hopeful about your present and future, and

• enjoy the pleasurable and beautiful things in life.

You probably will be able to achieve these in time. For most people, it takes not weeks, but months, or sometimes years. Current research indicates that for many survivors, bereavement following a sudden, violent death is very painful for three to four years.

Some people worry that they will forget their loved one if they begin to "get better." Stop worrying. You will never forget. You will always cherish the memory of your loved one. You will always be sorry you didn't share life with him or her for many more years. In time, however, you will remember the happy times more frequently than the painful ones that fill your mind now.

Stage Theories Don't Work

People have been writing about "stages of grief" as long as they have been talking about death, including sudden death. Most of us know about Elizabeth Kubler-Ross' stages: denial, anger, bargaining, depression, and acceptance. Dr. Ross' research was based primarily on children who were facing death in the future, and their parents. Morton Bard and Dawn Sangrey are early pioneers in research about crime victimization. They use these stages: initial disorganization or shock, struggle or recoil, and readjustment. Dr. Therese Rando, one of our country's finest contemporary grief researchers, speaks of three stages: avoidance, confrontation, and re-establishment.

"Stages" of grief can help us recognize components of grieving, but you must remember that stages are not firm, concrete, and predictable. They suggest trends that may help you to feel more normal as you read about them. However, they are to be understood as descriptive, not prescriptive. They become prescriptive if you start to believe that you are not grieving properly if you do not fit into a stage sequence. Over-emphasis on stages overlooks the totality of life. A "stage" may vary by month or by hour, and your reaction at any given time can be affected by what you are doing, who you are with, and a multitude of other circumstances.

You will best approach your trauma as a unique individual, recognizing that you are different from everyone else who experiences the same kind of trauma or a different one. The significance you place on this death, including what it can teach you, is unique only to you. Be gentle and patient with yourself. Later on, when you reach out to help others in similar circumstances, remember that their grief reaction will not be like yours. It is hurtful, for example, to try to push people from one "stage" to another. It's easy to think that "denial" or "shock" represents character weakness and that people should "face what happened." That's not necessarily true.

Common Reactions to Sudden Death

The following components are not "stages." They are components of the grief experience that many survivors experience from time to time. You may experience few or many of them. The important thing to remember, though, is that they are common.

Denial/Shock/Numbness

Denial is a wonderful thing. It is nature's way of warding off the full impact of trauma until a person is ready to absorb the totality of what happened. Most people, upon being told that a loved one has been killed, are rendered too weak to undertake the overwhelming task of grieving.

You may have gone into shock after learning what happened. Shock is similar to being given a general anesthetic. With the help of a quick spurt of adrenalin, endorphins, opiods, and other brain chemicals, you may have gone into primitive survivor mode. Your initial reaction may have been "fight," "flight," or "freeze." A hormone called oxytocin is secreted by both men and women under stress. Sometimes called "the cuddle hormone," it is the same one that women get huge spurts of after childbirth. It causes bonding and is partially the reason suddenly-bereaved people appreciate being touched and held. Researchers are finding that a woman's estrogen amplifies the effectiveness of oxytocin while a man's testosterone limits its action.

Experiencing any or all of these reactions does not mean that you are abnormal. If any of them become so pervasive that they significantly deter you from functioning, you may need some professional help. Otherwise, if you feel a little dissociated from yourself or if you feel rather disconnected, try to just let these reactions be. It is interesting that in times of war, when troops know the enemy is approaching, they take down street signs and markers, road signs, and other identifying indicators in order to confuse the enemy. You may feel like all the markers that have helped you find your way before are now absent. Don't worry. They will eventually return, and it is okay if you can't find them now.

If you stay in a state of high emotional arousal, though, perhaps feeling like you want to fight all the time, you may need some professional assistance to help you calm down. Police officers who deliver death notifications say it is not uncommon for survivors to go into primitive survival mode. Some who tend to be "fighters" under stress may physically attack the person who delivers the death message. Those whose stress reaction is "flight" may faint or run to escape the situation. The term "frozen fright" is used to describe those unable to react.

"It was 12:30 AM on June 10th when the call came from the hospital telling me that my son, John, had been injured. Because I was alone, the police came to pick me up. All the way to Massachusetts General, the two officers in front talked about trivial matters. Neither of them spoke a word to me. When we got to the hospital, I was questioned about insurance and then put in a room by myself.

I sat alone reciting the Hail Mary aloud to break the silence and tension. Eventually, a young doctor, obviously tired and aggravated, entered the room, hopped up on a gurney, and said, 'Your son has expired.' That's all.

'I don't know what to say,' I stammered, as if I could ever be prepared for such an event. I ran from the hospital, and outside, screamed and screamed and screamed."

– Margaret Grogan, whose son, John
was stabbed in the heart at
a graduation party

"I prayed all the way to the hospital, 'Please God, at least give him five more minutes.' But it was too late. Since I'm a registered nurse, I've had to tell people that their child was dead. It's something that you never get used to. But I never dreamed I would walk into an emergency room and have my husband tell me, 'Oh God, Sally, our baby is dead.' I watched a nice man dissolve before my eyes. I felt my 15-year-old son hitting on me, begging me to say his brother wasn't dead. I watched my daughter crumble and say, 'Mom, I want to get the guy who did this.'"

– Sally Jeanes, whose 18-year-old
son, Jason, was killed by a drunk driver

Regardless of the initial impact, if you are like most people, you soon found yourself in a state of numbness. Looking back on it now, you may wonder how you remained calm. You may have completed some tasks that now seem impossible. You probably have a hard time remembering exactly what you did during those first few days.

"I was having trouble making sense of it all, and nurses were staring at me. I didn't want to think about the boys and what had happened to them. I was alive. Maybe they were, too. Words seemed to hang in the air while I tried to make sense of them. Words like 'dead' and 'autopsy' floated through the air. I didn't want to hear them. But all I could say was, 'Please don't tell me how many of them are dead.'"

– Betty Jane Spencer, recalling her condition
before being told that her four sons had been killed

During this time, people often comment on how "strong" you are. One of the saddest parts of trauma is that people assume you are strong when your brain has simply put you on hold. You may appear strong, but you feel like a mechanical robot. When the shock wears off and you desperately need your friends, they may have resumed life as usual, believing that you are doing fine and don't need any more support.

> "For the first few months, I was in a daze. I was plagued by flashbacks, but I only half believed it was real. Friends commented on how brave and calm and strong I was. What they did not know was that I had not yet fully comprehended the enormity of what had happened."
>
> *– Barbara Kaplan, who was seriously*
> *injured, but survived a shooting in which*
> *two of her friends were killed*

This sense of feeling that you are disconnected from yourself and others is natural and functional. It is important that you travel through this part of grief at you own pace and try not to worry about it. It will serve you well until you are stronger and better able to cope.

Some people may think that something is wrong with you and try to force you into facing reality. It is impossible to push through any component of grieving simply to "get it over with." If you cannot think clearly, if you seem forgetful, and if you feel detached, be patient with yourself. If you need help with essential tasks, ask for it. However, be very careful about using alcohol or sedating prescriptive drugs. They can push you into an unnatural sense of detachment. Allow your own body to compensate for the trauma.

Fear/Vulnerability

Many family members are surprised to find that they feel anxious, fearful, and powerless in the aftermath of a sudden death. Although you knew that tragedies occurred, you may have believed that they happened to other people. Before your trauma, you may have felt uniquely invulnerable. It wouldn't happen to you.

After your loved one was killed, you may have felt that life was so "out of kilter" that you found yourself waiting for another shoe to drop. It's strange how we tend to believe that good things happen to good people and bad thing happen to bad people. That belief, for you, is now proven false.

You may feel that you and your remaining loved ones are more vulnerable to trouble than other people. You will need to think rationally and work hard to risk going out into crowds even when it frightens you. Little by little, you can overcome these fears. It is maddening to realize that the killer not only destroyed your loved one, but also damaged the part of you that was previously confident and carefree.

> "The fact that I could be killed hit me with full force. I felt powerless and off-balance. Would I feel frightened of everyone I didn't know? I saw each stranger as a potential killer. I envied those who walked trusting others. I worried about becoming weak and fearful."
> – *Jean Goldberg*

> "If you think about it, everything we do in life depends on others acting in a rational and predictable way. When you get in a car and drive it away, you're investing a lot of trust in every other driver on the road. So, what happens when that trust is gone? Try driving down a two-lane highway with cars passing you just a few feet over in the oncoming lane. Your guts will be in knots if you can handle it at all. When you start to see every faceless stranger as a potential madman or thug, you're not only scared, but depressed. You really feel betrayed!"
> – *Barbara Kaplan*

"Since that week, I feel differently about life. I don't feel so young. I'm 27, but after losing my 4-year-old son, I know there's nothing fair about death. I often think it could happen again. I think of death often. I told my mother the other day that I'll miss her when she dies."

– Kim Keyes, whose child, Kurt, was killed in an automobile crash along with three other relatives and a family friend.

The vulnerability of knowing that tragedy can strike anyone at any time has an almost existential quality. It leads to questions like, "What is life, anyhow?" "What are we here for?" "Why do people have to die?" "Why didn't God do something to stop it?" These issues can be doubly overwhelming to adolescents who are just beginning to try to figure out life, let alone death. Facing the pain in the household can be so uncomfortable that young people may seek ways to escape rather than face their own vulnerability.

Aches, Pains, and Illness

Traumatic stress can make you physically sick. As you experience sadness, confusion, fear, anxiety, and anger, you may find that you have no appetite. You may feel weak, as if you can't take another step. You may feel exhausted, but when you go to bed, you can't sleep or you sleep only a short time. Your sex drive may be gone or diminished.

Many survivors speak of heaviness in their chest, a symptom some refer to as "a broken heart." You may feel nervous and edgy. You may have stomachaches or headaches.

If these ailments escalate, some people begin to think about suicide as a means of relief. They wish they could die, too, to escape the pain. Friends and relatives who care about you are crucially important to your well-being at these times. Lean on them, especially those who know how to listen. They can help you think rationally about what is best for you and your family.

You may need to see a doctor, especially if you are not eating, not sleeping, and spending a great deal of time wishing you were dead. Even if your symptoms are not this severe, your immune system may be compromised by the stress, which makes you more vulnerable to disease.

Many grieving people become accident-prone. They have automobile accidents, fall frequently, and experience other mishaps. These can happen when you are preoccupied with your loss.

If you are vulnerable to cardiovascular disease or other serious illnesses, you must have regular checkups. Some research has suggested a correlation between grief and the onset of cancer.

If you use tobacco or drugs, including alcohol, you will need to very carefully monitor your use. Some grieving people increase their usage in order to escape and to sleep. This leads to serious problems. Alcohol is a depressant. It increases rather than decreases grief. It aggravates other physical conditions. It disrupts rather than enhances sleep. Grieving, as painful as it is, is usually best leaned into and fully experienced. Alcohol and other drugs help only for a few hours. Then you feel worse.

Your doctor may prescribe medication to help you eat or sleep during the initial phase of grieving. Do not consider this a weakness. You have suffered severe trauma and deserve this help to begin feeling better. You will probably need prescribed antidepressant or anti-anxiety medication for a short time only. Even if you don't want to feel better yet, you owe it to yourself and your family to stay in good health.

Anger

You may be surprised at the intensity of anger you feel toward the person who killed your loved one, even if it was a suicide. The more senseless the act, the more angry you may feel. Some survivors do not feel angry, but most do, some to the point of rage.

"I didn't think it was possible to hate someone so much. I felt the most deep, penetrating hate I have ever known in my life. I'm a pastor, and it's pretty shocking to find out the kinds of feeling one can have."
  – *Tinka Bloedow, whose 14-year-old daughter, Tee Ja, was killed by a drunk driver.*

You may wish desperately that the person who killed your loved one would show some remorse or say, "I'm sorry." That probably won't happen.

Many offenders do not appear to feel remorse. Some are indeed sorry. Their attorneys, however, will warn them to make no contact with you because such contact can be considered an admission of guilt.

Some people experience anger early in their grieving. Others feel angry later, after some of the numbness has worn off. You may have been angry before you were willing to admit it.

It is unfortunate that most of us were taught as children that some feelings are bad. Most of us heard:

- "You shouldn't get angry."
- "It's wrong to feel jealous."
- "It's sinful to think about vengeance."
- "Rage is a terrible thing."

Feelings are not right or wrong. They simply are. Your behavior may be good or bad, right or wrong, appropriate or not appropriate. Your thinking may be clear or foggy, rational or irrational. However, your feelings are simply your feelings with no "shoulds" attached. It is silly of people to suggest that you should stop having a particular feeling. It is impossible just to will a feeling to stop.

"It might comfort victims, especially those who feel cheated by the criminal justice system, to know that it is acceptable and helpful to fantasize about the 'justice' they would like to impose on the killer. One of the most helpful things I learned in coping was that feelings are involuntary, like the urge to sneeze, and can seldom be suppressed. Even the most negative of angry thoughts and feelings are not wrong. 'Wrong' comes in only if they translate into behaviors."

– Janet Barton, whose son was murdered

It is very important that you not act destructively in response to your anger. You must force yourself to think rationally about what you can do with your anger that will not hurt anyone. But what you feel is what you feel.

You may find yourself angry not only at the person who killed your loved one, but at God, at the doctors, at investigating officers, and even at your family. You may be angry at everyone who seems to be going on with life as if nothing happened. You may even be angry at your dead loved one for abandoning you, no matter how much you know it wasn't his or her fault. Obviously, such anger is misplaced, and should not be acted out.

"And there is anger. My anger didn't stop at God or at the murderers. I hated everything and everyone. It was a raw, ugly, destructive feeling that could rise in me and control me for days on end."

– Betty Jane Spencer, whose four sons were murdered

The injustice of your loved one's death, the deep hurt you feel, and the loss of future dreams may all add up to rage, a wordless drive to do something. Most of the things you think about doing, however, must remain as thoughts. Try not to act on your rage.

"I fantasized for a year about going into the courtroom and blowing his head off, but I decided to leave it all in

God's hands. Things have a way of turning out."
– June Sanborn, whose only child, Diane, was murdered
by choking, stabbing, and sexual mutilation

It's okay to think about it, and it's very helpful to talk about it with someone who is willing to listen. If you can find another person who has felt somewhat as you do to talk with, you are very fortunate.

Sadly, many friends, and even relatives, will not be willing to listen as you ventilate intense feelings. Their discomfort and negative reactions can make you even more angry. It would be helpful if others could understand that expressing strong feelings means that you are taking responsibility for them and are not likely to act on them. You may need to explain this to those who don't seem to understand.

Allowing yourself to express these feelings will probably free your mind, enabling you to be more realistic in your thinking and constructive in your planning for the future.

Anger manifests itself physically as well as emotionally. If you suppress anger, or try to prevent yourself from feeling it, you may develop problems in your body. Symptoms can include headaches, stomach aches, colitis, backaches, high blood pressure, and others.

On the other hand, positive physical activity often helps. Some people run, others exercise vigorously, and some clean house. Vigorous exercise releases many brain chemicals that can calm and soothe. It can even decrease depression.

Others keep a journal or write letters to the offender (which are usually best unmailed). Some cry, yell, and scream. Common places for this kind of emotional release are in the shower and in the car. What you do with your anger really doesn't matter, as long as you admit that it's there and you don't hurt yourself or anyone else when expressing it.

You may find that your anger is serving a somewhat useful purpose. Deep sadness may be lurking beneath the anger. While anger does not feel good, it is usually less painful than sadness. Anger is generally focused on someone else, but it can sometimes be splattered on a wide spectrum, not seeming to attach to anyone or anything for long. Sadness is more often focused inside yourself. You will eventually need to give up some of the anger, rage and vengeance and face the sad feelings underneath.

When you decide to discover what's beneath the anger, you may find loneliness and longing. It may be guilt. It can be most anything. By being willing to face it, however, you may find relief from your anger. You may think that you owe it to your loved one to remain angry. That doesn't make sense. However, what you do with your anger, and when you decide to look beneath it are up to you.

This somewhat confused society of ours seems to tell us in print, on television, and in the movies that anger should be ventilated at all cost. Research has not found that to be so. In fact, those who spend much of their lives spewing anger are more likely than others to get sick. The goal is not just to ventilate anger, but to name the emotional reaction that feels so bad and see if something constructive can be done with it.

As someone recently said, "Blowing your stack simply pollutes the air. It accomplishes nothing."

For example, you may learn that the prosecutor is contemplating a plea bargain, which you do not understand, and that he has no plan to consult you about it. That may be enough to enrage you. But, before you pick up the phone, ask yourself, "How can I get what I want?" Throwing a fit in the prosecutor's office or writing a nasty "Letter to the Editor" is more likely to alienate than to get what you want.

Instead, call the prosecutor and ask for a fifteen-minute appointment to discuss the case. If the appointment is granted, calmly ask the prosecutor to help you understand his reasoning for considering the plea rather than pursuing a conviction on the original charges. Sometimes, there is a very good reason for offering a plea bargain. In several states, for example, murder is being charged in serious drunk driving death cases. The legal elements required to secure a murder conviction are complex. Perhaps, as the investigation is carried out, the prosecutor discovers that not all the necessary elements can be proven. In such a case, it is better to accept a guilty plea to a lesser offense than to risk losing everything. If it's a judgment call, some prosecutors may proceed to trial if you feel strongly about it. You may be willing to risk losing the case in order to risk winning. However, the prosecutor retains ultimate discretion in the decision. Some will not go to trial because they do not want to risk acquittals on their records. In any event, you may feel a sense of relief if you discuss your concerns with the prosecutor.

Post-Traumatic Stress/Guilt

For a long time, it was believed that most of the painful stress that people feel comes from within. Depressed people were thought to have serious internal conflicts that needed to be worked out.

Now, we understand that external trauma is a valid basis for significant distress. While this understanding may or may not help you feel better, it is actually good news. It is good news because it means that you are not "crazy" just because you are experiencing very painful symptoms in the aftermath of your loved one's death. These symptoms are the result of something that happened outside yourself, not inside yourself.

> "According to the religion I was raised in, if anything bad happened to you, it was somehow your own fault through sin or whatever. A very valuable thing that therapy taught me was that what happened was external, not brought on by something in my own heart."
>
> – *Mary Walker, who experienced the traumatic deaths of three of her children on separate occasions*

As denial and shock wear off, you may experience some reactions that are foreign and frightening. You may find that particular images of the trauma keep intruding into your mind. They may be particular sights, sounds, or smells. You may have repeated nightmares. Something may make you feel as if the trauma is happening again. If you are aware of what initiates these reactions, the site of the death, a certain song, specific events, you may almost compulsively avoid those things, somewhat like a phobia.

You may feel that the external world doesn't have much meaning anymore. You may feel like withdrawing because it seems that no one understands your pain. You may have difficulty concentrating, feeling absent-minded and confused.

The Mother Lode

A single eye blazing in my forehead,
I mine your death.
Sifting through the layers,
hording every glint.

Here,
a pile of undone dreams.
And here,
a mound of guilt, if onlys,
blasted touch.
My fossil love.

Blackened with loss,
deeper and deeper
I dig
for the mother lode.
    – Anita Huffington, whose daughter was killed

You may struggle with guilt: "If only I had _____" becomes a familiar theme for nearly all family members and close friends following homicide or suicide.

Human beings tend to believe a lot of things that don't make sense when examined closely. For instance:

- People who love each other should always be responsible for each other and be able to protect each other.

- If I had been a better person, this wouldn't have happened.

- If I begin to feel better it will mean that I didn't love him/her enough.

- It is not right that my loved one died and I continue to live.

You may find that when you cry, beneath the tears are the words, "I'm sorry, I'm sorry, I'm sorry." Perhaps you feel guilty because you still believe the old adage, "Good things happen to good people and bad things happen to bad people." It may seem that if you can just find a way to prove that you were guilty (bad), at least you can hang on to an old belief that you perceive makes some sense of your loved one's death.

One of the most difficult tasks of mourning is to look rationally at why your beliefs make you feel guilty. You may, indeed, be responsible for some component of your loved one's death. If so, acknowledge it and see if you can find a way to forgive yourself. If you made a bad judgment, you probably made the best one you knew how to make at the time. Try not to exaggerate your role in what happened, because doing that will confuse you.

In most cases, other factors were largely responsible for your loved one's death. The person who killed your loved one either chose to do so or was negligent in such a way that the death happened. Forces of nature also play a role. One law of nature is that when two powerful, opposing forces collide, one or both are destroyed. It would be nice, maybe, if such laws did not always work. On the other hand, it would be frightening to live in a world where nature's laws sometimes worked and sometimes didn't.

You may conclude, by thinking rationally, that you were 5% responsible and someone else was 95% responsible. In that case, take on only 5% of the guilt, not 100%.

Talking with others who understand some of what you're going through can help you look at your guilt realistically. Feeling less guilty won't take away your sadness or your anger, but it can be a big load off your shoulders. It will be worth the effort to lesson your burden, but it will be hard work.

Acknowledgment/Accommodation

The word "acceptance" is not used here because the sudden, violent killing of someone you love is never "acceptable." In the beginning, some people believe they will never be happy again. They go through a period of time when they aren't ready to feel better. Others are eager to feel better and work to find ways to do it.

Whether you are ready to feel better or not, you might want to look to others who have survived a similar ordeal and have managed to regain strength and find happiness again. They can be encouraging models.

It is a fact that your life will never be the same as it was before your loved one was killed. However, it probably will be a lot better than it is now as you read this book.

Acknowledging what happened means believing that it happened as it did, based on all you can learn about it. It means you no longer have to pretend it did not happen in the manner it did. It means being willing to face and experience the pain rather than avoiding it by over-activism or escape into alcohol or other drugs. It means deciding how to live with your memories.

Memories can never be taken from you, even though other people may tell you that you should move on. Thomas Attig describes the grief process as one of "loving others in their presence" to "loving them in their absence," creating a "place in the heart" where memory is freely stored and easily accessed.

> "When my son died, they gave me some peace lilies from his funeral and I planted them out back. Now there are about twenty of them. When my momma died, I planted a gardenia in his garden. The other day I was getting out of the car in front of the house, and all of a sudden, I smelled the gardenia, but I couldn't see any flowers. I said, 'Momma, where are you? I can smell you, but I can't see you.' Then I pulled back a branch, and there was the first gardenia flower of spring. I said, 'Well, hello, Momma! Don't you look beautiful this morning!'"
>
> *– Mrs. Dixon, whose granddaughter was*
> *murdered, and whose son was murdered*
> *the following year*

You may be afraid you will forget memories that you don't want to forget. Many people find it helpful to write down six to ten especially wonderful memories. Get them out and read them often. You may want to save other mementos with your writings such as a lock of hair, perfume, aftershave, or pieces of clothing. Use these from time to time to cherish the memory. Remind yourself of the good memories when you feel yourself slipping into pain again. Begin to recognize the parts of your loved one that are now incorporated into yourself and other family members.

Your experience can trigger not only post-traumatic stress, but post-traumatic growth as well, as you begin to reconstruct your own identity. You may discover a new appreciation for life and more sensitivity to others.

> "Accommodation comes when you decide you care whether your own life continues or not. I will never

forget Trey, and I will look forward to seeing him in Heaven, but I am going on with my life here, and I find joy in it."

— Ralph Shelton, whose son was shot and killed by a sniper

Sorrow

You will always feel sorrow that your loved one died tragically and that the long relationship you might have enjoyed was cut short. However, this very appropriate sense of sorrow differs significantly from the depth of trauma that most family members experience for the first few months.

Sorrow's parameters are not clear. Some people describe the sorrow as a "misty fog on life," of which they are not always aware. They simply realize that life is not quite as bright, not quite as light as it was before. Values change. You may now find yourself impatient with trivia. You may feel misunderstood. However, a sense of sorrow is not the same as being overwhelmed with grief or depression.

"Every time I tell our story, I feel cleansed when it is finished. It's important that people know what a neat kid Kurt was. For the first months, we dwelled on things we didn't do with Kurt. Now we think of things we did do. It's more positive. You need to celebrate what their lives meant to you."

— Kim Keyes, whose 4-year-old son, Kurt, was killed by a drunk driver

Grief Spasms

It is likely that you will experience sudden grief spasms from time to time over the years. Survivors are often surprised to find that even in the midst of a series of good days, something brings on a spasm of grief. Anniversaries often are difficult; the birthday of the loved one, the anniversary of the death, the wedding anniversary,

Mother's Day, Father's Day. Holidays in which family togetherness is a tradition are often difficult for families experiencing sudden loss. Certain songs can cause a grief spasm. Seeing someone who resembles your loved one can bring on a grief spasm.

Strange as it may seem, though, grief spasms can be understood as celebrations of a relationship that meant so much to you that episodes of grief can still overcome you.

Nearly all family members are able to say that they would rather have shared life with their loved one as long as they did than not at all. Being able to experience the depth of sadness and the height of joy is to be fully alive, fully human. Most people are glad they are capable of having strong feelings. Experiencing the strong feelings means that shock symptoms and numbness are no longer necessary, and fullness of the experience of the trauma can be absorbed.

As time goes by, grief spasms will come less frequently and less intensely. Most survivors are able to acknowledge that their loved one would want it that way.

Your loved one would want to be fondly remembered from time to time, and even missed. But if you remain caught up in a chronic sense of desperation, the possibility of more set-backs could evolve. That would benefit no one and would not be the wish of your loved one.

> "On some days I'm fine. Then something will happen and I will be right back where I was. I don't cry as much as I did in the beginning. But I don't laugh as much as I did before the crash either. I feel like part of me will never come back. But I want it to come back."
> – Sally Jeanes, whose 18-year-old son,
> Jason, was killed by a drunk driver

Focus on Life

Another component of acknowledgment or "getting better" is an increasing focus on life and a decreasing focus on death. Early on, you may have felt that you barely existed. Others who told you to cheer up and get on with your life may have seemed unwilling to share your grief journey. They may have been uncomfortable around you.

You may be disappointed with family and friends for their lack of sensitivity and understanding. Some employers and faith communities are even worse. They can make you frustrated and angry. However, you will have to decide for yourself when it is right to give more of your attention to living. You can use your grief to continue to drag you down or you can use it to rebuild your life, probably with more compassion and understanding than you had before.

Think about the person you were before this tragedy happened. How would you have described your values and strengths? That same person still lives! He or she has been damaged, but the core person remains. We are re-shaped by our traumas, but we are still much more than our traumas.

> "You don't have to remain a victim. It's your choice. One day, I realized I could focus on the fact that I was surviving rather than on how much I was diminished by Adrianne's murder. I was getting up in the morning and going to bed at night. I felt I was living, no longer controlled by the tragedy."
> *– Linda Jones, whose daughter was*
> *shot and killed*

By having experienced trauma, you eventually will be able to keep life in perspective better than other people. After suffering, many people seem to develop a peace, sensitivity, and inner wisdom that others lack.

"I feel almost invincible. I have survived the worst thing that could happen. All other problems pale in comparison. If I could survive that, I can survive anything."

> *– Ralph Shelton, whose son was shot and killed by a sniper*

Call to Justice

In some cases, enduring trauma ignites a spark of activity to right some of the wrongs associated with sudden violent deaths. Most survivors want to prevent it for others.

Thousands of men, women, and teenagers have joined *Mothers Against Drunk Driving* after the death of a loved one at the hands of a drunk driver. Their desire is to help other injured victims and survivors cope emotionally, to help them through the criminal justice system, and to prevent drunken driving crashes.

After their daughter, Lisa, was killed, Charlotte and Bob Hullinger founded *Parents of Murdered Children* as a support for other families forced to endure such tragedy.

The Compassionate Friends has support groups in most communities around the country where parents of children who have died comfort each other.

Rabbi Harold Kushner wrote the book, *When Bad Things Happen to Good People*, after his son died. He has continued to write other helpful books for people in difficult situations.

Not all survivors choose to undertake such large and noble tasks. Some reach out in smaller ways. After their daughter, Sarah, was killed in Seattle, Tom and Mary Yarborough opened a bed & breakfast especially for grieving people. Most people who endure tragedies eventually become willing, even eager, to touch others who are surviving similar losses. By doing so, they offer one of the most treasured gifts a human being can give to another.

Suggestions

Understand that the shock and injustice of losing someone you love to a sudden, violent, and senseless death can result in grief with a wide range and depth of reactions. Your grief may last longer than that for survivors of anticipated, non-violent death. If you are coping well, wonderful! However, if you are having a hard time, be patient with yourself. Many people struggle for months and years before they feel a resolution of their grieving.

- Maintain regular contact with your physician for several years to be sure that you do not acquire a stress-related physical condition.

- Try to delay major decisions such as moving, remarrying, having a baby, or changing jobs for at least a year. No matter how positive they seem, major decisions create additional stress.

- Feel your feelings, whether they are sadness, rage, or vengeance. Find a way to express them, perhaps through writing letters or in a journal, sharing with someone else, or through physical activity. Try to think rationally and to act responsibly.

- Take a realistic look at any guilt you feel. If you are guilty in part for what happened, try to forgive yourself. If God can forgive you, can't you? Do not carry a load of guilt that is not appropriate for what happened.

- Try to understand family members who may be grieving differently. It is rare for any two people in a family to handle trauma the same way. Remember that there are no rules for how one should grieve. Try to talk about what you are feeling and encourage others to do the same. Attempt to receive what you hear, even though your experience may be different.

• Be patient with others who say inept things to you. Very rarely are these comments intended to hurt you. While most people want to help you, they may not know what to say or do. Try to be grateful for their attempt, if not for the end result.

• Remember that no one can fill the shoes of the loved one who has died. It is unrealistic to think that another person or activities can fill the vacuum now in your heart. Expecting another person to fulfill you places a terrible burden on him or her.

• Seek the support and understanding of others who have gone through similar traumas. You and your family can benefit from the assistance of others. Call your local Mental Health Association, hospice, and/or clergy to locate support groups and professional counselors who understand the grief that follows your unique loss and trauma. Review the Resources section at the end of this book and contact national organizations that interest you to identify your nearest local affiliate. You do not have to handle this alone.

• Find a way to make a positive contribution from your tragedy. This does not mean imposing your memories or experience on newly bereaved people. They will ask you to share your experience when they are ready to hear it. It means making yourself available to them on their terms. Affiliating with action-oriented organizations is one way to reach out to others.

• Remember that you are much more than your trauma. Your core values and strengths are still the real you.

• Realize that getting better does not mean that you didn't love your loved one enough. Nor does it mean that you will forget him or her. When and how you begin to feel better and what your pilgrimage toward recovery is like, are up to you.

What I Want to Remember From This Chapter

Chapter Three

DEATH OF A DAUGHTER OR SON

Couples as Parents

As a parent, you probably spent much of your time thinking about how to protect your children and nurture them into adulthood. As they grew into late adolescence, you had to figure out how to "let them go" into their own adulthood.

When parenting is successful, you expect your children, as adults themselves, to continue to love you, but you do not expect them to remain dependent on you. In fact, as you become older, you may depend on your children to care for you. In time, you expect to die and be survived by your children. When your child dies, every one of those expectations is aborted.

The way you nurture a child is different from the way you care for a mate, parents, or friends. When your child is very young, he is totally dependent on you. One amazing thing about human nature is that nurturing a baby, toddler, or a young child is as fulfilling for the parent as it is for the child. That is true, however, only if the parent is emotionally healthy. Emotionally inadequate parents sometimes abuse or neglect their children.

If you are a healthy parent, you are so bonded to your young child that comforting him and keeping him content also makes you comfortable and content. The emptiness that remains when you no longer have your child to nurture can be so painful that some have referred to it as a chronic physical ache.

"This space is within me all the time it seems. Sometimes the empty space is so real I can almost touch it. I can almost see it. It gets so big sometimes I can't see anything else."

– Mary Sennewald

As children grow older, they develop a sense of themselves that is separate from their parents. This need to separate is a normal part of child development. New behaviors during this stage require parents to guide and appropriately discipline the child. Most parents may feel an even stronger need to protect their child as they see him or her grow up.

All children make mistakes. It is hard for a parent to decide when to step in and protect the child, and when to let the child learn by experiencing the consequences of his mistakes. Parents are strongly driven, however, to protect their child from serious harm, no matter how old the child. If they had the choice, most parents would rather die themselves than endure the serious injury or death of their child.

A very difficult part of grieving for most parents whose child has been killed is the fact that they were not able to protect their child. You may feel extremely angry with yourself for not preventing the tragedy. You may feel guilty, as if the child's death was your fault, even if you know it was not.

All day long, I listen for his step,
his whistle, his sweet, uncertain song.
I listen until the silence tightens
around my throat.

Oh God, you know I'd give my life
to hear his voice again.
To feel, once more, the touch of his
young, eager hand.

To stand and watch him play,
and feel the pride leap in me like a flame.

I'd give my life, I say,
and yet I wouldn't.
I must stay here
and do my job
until I've earned the right to go away.
– Elsie Robinson

Coping with the death of an older child is different from coping with the death of a young child. Parents may not love older children less, but their life experiences with them are different. As children become older, they take more risks, check out more unknown territory, and try to solve their own problems. All of that is a very normal part of adolescent development. These phrases probably have a familiar ring to parents of teenagers.

"I've got to be me!"

"You have got to let me grow up!"

"Get off my back. Weren't you ever a teenager?"

You may recall your child stomping out of the room or slamming doors. Parents are usually resistant to these kinds of words and behaviors. That, too, is normal. While the push and pull of raising a teenager is not always pleasant, it is a sign that the teen is seeking and discovering his own values. That is good.

When an older child dies, parents may have a very difficult time realizing that they were doing the right thing by allowing their child to take risks. If you chose to allow your child some freedom, and it resulted in your child's death, it will not help to place all the blame on yourself. You probably made the best decision you knew how to make at the time.

So many recollections bring you to me,
Your insistence on being just you.
"Stubborn," we said.
But no, you were "right."
You knew what you wanted since age two.

Friends, problems, college life, romance from afar,
Sorority joys, world troubles, future dreams,
"Mom, don't expect grandkids or even marriage for
awhile... maybe never."
You prepared me it seems.
Thank you, Valerie, for being our daughter.
Your mother and dad love you so.
We didn't tell you that very often.
So, now, our tears must let you know.
     – Katherine D. Guayante, in memory of Valerie

Another component of grieving when a child has been killed has to do with your investment, which has now come to naught. You invested heavily in your child emotionally. Even if you faced difficult days with your child, you developed dreams for his future. As your child grew older, you noted special talents and interests. Your child may have spent time talking with you about what she wanted to be or do upon growing up.

You probably invested financially in those dreams. You purchased insurance policies to ensure that your child would have enough money when you die. You may have paid for braces, for music lessons. You may have encouraged your child to develop skills in sports or other physical activities. You may have bought computers or other technological equipment to help your child achieve. You may have borrowed money or set aside funds to help your child through college.

Parents would gladly pay it all again, and a thousand times over, if they could have their child back. That isn't possible. It may help, however, to understand that your financial investment was symbolic of your emotional investment. It may help you understand why a child's death seems so deeply wrong.

To face the death of a child is not only to lose someone you feel driven to nurture and protect, but also to lose hopes and dreams for the future.

> "No words can ever describe the pain of losing a child. On that night in April, a large part of my inner self died along with my only daughter. All of her hopes and dreams are gone. She will never graduate from high school, go to college, or experience the special love of a husband and children. All those things she spoke of so often are gone, and with them so much of my future. The void will be with me the rest of my life."
> *– Ginger Babb, whose 17-year-old daughter, Julie, who was killed*

Couples as Mates

The death of a child can make a significant impact on the marriage of the parents. Some couples find that the tragedy draws them closer together. This can happen when they communicate openly and support each other as first one, and then the other, has good days and then bad days. It is common, however, for relationships to suffer in the aftermath of a tragedy so great as the death of a child.

It is very difficult to support and nurture your mate when your own grief is so overwhelming. When experiencing trauma, many people regress to a somewhat childlike state. They feel vulnerable and need to be taken care of. If both mates are in the same condition, and neither has the strength to care for the other, feelings of alienation can emerge.

> This morning, upon my husband's pillow,
> A tear.
> Last night I heard no weeping,

I felt no rhythmic shaking.
Yet there it is,
Glistening, silent testimony to pain.

Quickly I reached to blot it,
As if one swift brush
Could set the world right again.
But something stops my hand,
Stops me to wonder:
Am I the cause of weeping?

In my life is much sorrow,
Dreadful longing, and much emptiness
That even my husband cannot fill.
Sorrow brings sleepless nights in fear
Of other phone calls and ambulances;
More longing and emptiness.
My husband shares this loss
But men don't cry.
They nod gravely and tend to details,
Make arrangements and give support.
Yet, there it is upon his pillow:
A tear.

Have I given way to grief
And forgotten one who shares?
Have I made no room for his tears
In the flood of mine?
Am I the reason he weeps
Only in the silence of the night?

I close my hand
To leave the tear drying there.
No more will I blot out his pain
To tend to mine,
For we must share
In order to live, together.
        – *Marcia Alig*

Because your drive to nurture and protect has been violently interrupted, you may have a strong need to blame. As previously discussed, many parents blame themselves and feel guilty. It is also tempting to blame your mate.

When a child develops a terminal illness, it is usually no one's fault. Parents can become very angry that science has not found a cure or that treatment was not successful. However, as parents care for their child through the dying process, they know that they did everything they could.

When a child is killed, someone usually was at fault. If the cause of the death is not explicitly clear, parents may engage in a relentless search for answers. They can usually find a way to blame the other parent, at least in part.

Blaming intensifies the impact of the trauma. While women often need to communicate in order to feel better, men tend to withdraw to feel better. Men and women certainly receive different messages from our culture about how to react to significant losses, but recent research has revealed actual chemical differences that contribute to the different styles of coping. Rarely do two people move through grieving in the same way. One partner may be angry, deeply resenting the loss of control over the child's life and death and choose to ventilate those reactions privately, or even engage in aggressive behavior. The other mate may be more open, needing to talk about it, to cry with someone who understands. This partner may be more sorrowful and wonder how the other has the energy to be so angry. On another day, these roles may be reversed.

One of you may cry at the mention, or even the thought, of the child who has been killed. The other may function well enough to return to work. One may read books to better understand what is happening to them, while the other may refuse to face the tragedy. One may want to go to a support group of fellow sufferers while the other withdraws at the mention of it. It is very difficult to understand and accept each other's grieving when they are so different.

65

"I felt different emotions than my husband did. I felt compassion for the other driver, feeling his conscience would punish him. My husband wanted him to pay dearly. Then there was, for a time, so much guilt. If Mike had just had a bigger, faster car, a daytime job, so many 'ifs.' My husband seemed to have a larger problem with this than I did. I only wished I had said 'I love you' more often."

— *Rita Chiavacci*

A very practical side of these differences has to do with deciding what to do with the child's "things." One parent may be eager to dismantle the child's room and discard clothing and mementos. The other may believe that to do so would deny the existence of the child. Trying to find a happy medium for these polarities may be difficult.

Many couples are distressed to learn that jealousy and envy rear their ugly heads during grieving. If you spend your days at home, depressed and apathetic, you may envy your mate who is at work because you fantasize that he or she can be happy there with the many distractions that a job entails. If you are the one working, you may envy the mate at home who can face the grief and not have to "hold up" to get the job done.

The father may envy the mother because she carried the child in her body for nine months and birthed it, a closeness with which he is unable to identify.

Mates may have unrealistic expectations of each other regarding workload and maintenance of the home. Sloppy housekeeping or failure to mow the lawn may infuriate a mate who is depending on the other to stay on top of things. Many couples say it takes months before they have enough energy to do more than what simply has to be done.

Sexuality can become a divisive issue during bereavement. Your mate may face an increased need for sex as nurture, escape, or release, while you are repulsed at the thought of it. Avoidance of sex can stem from fear of having and losing other children. It can be rooted in guilt over experiencing pleasure when something so awful has happened. It can also manifest as a classic symptom of depression.

When your barriers to feelings are let down in order to experience sexual intimacy, then the floodgate is also opened to pain and grief. Since sexual intimacy and orgasm can put you in touch with feelings at a deep level, you many avoid it for fear of tapping into uncontrollable painful emotional release. This can be complicated by the fact that your mate may have mannerisms or physical attributes similar to that of the dead child. To be reminded so potently of your child's death when approaching sexual intimacy can be devastating.

Any of these problems can cause you or your mate to back away from sexual contact. Then the avoidance, if not talked about, can be perceived as additional rejection. For example, your mate may perceive you as unresponsive and totally wrapped up in your grief when you say you are not interested in sex. Your mate may then perceive you as insensitive to his or her needs. In fact, both of you are hurting and simply trying to minimize your pain.

Unfortunately, your mate is the most readily accessible target for venting all types of frustrations. You spend many hours together. Your defenses are down more at home than anywhere else. It is important for you to understand that these problems nearly always arise. You will be fortunate if they do not.

When these issues do surface, try to understand that they are normal consequences of your child's death. You don't feel normal. However, you are normal in the sense that pain and struggle following major surgery are normal. A very significant part of your life has been cut out. The process of getting better requires time, patience, and effort.

An oft-quoted myth is that 80% to 90% of marriages fail when a child dies. Studies reaching this conclusion failed to take normal divorce rates into account and were based on couples already in counseling when their child died. We now know that when divorce does follow the death of a child, it is usually because of problems in the marriage before the death. Perhaps the marital problems no longer seem reconcilable after the death of the child. Some of the positive aspects of living through trauma, reordered priorities, a sense of endurance, and newfound assertiveness, may contribute to the decision to go ahead and divorce. In fact, most marriages do survive the death of a child.

How Long Will It Take?

You are no longer the same person you were before your child died. To expect that you will ever be exactly the same is to place an unrealistic burden on yourself. It is also impossible to place a timetable on your grieving. Remember that many factors play into grief, and each person develops his or her own timetable.

Some parents begin to feel better as they are able to make sense of what happened through learning all the facts. Some begin to feel better after the court case is completed. It is not that justice makes what happened acceptable. However, a reasonable justice outcome does represent an end to one chapter in a book of challenges.

Some people say that the second year is harder than the first. Most people feel noticeably better by the third or fourth year, although some find the third year more difficult than the second. Research shows that most survivors feel significantly better by the fourth year. There will always be good days and bad days, but the pain decreases as time goes on. You will one day be surprised to realize that you can feel sad without becoming engulfed in grief. You will again be happy, if only for short periods of time at first. Having friends and family who love you and accept you as you are is a blessing. They may be more important than anyone else in helping you heal.

You may want to keep a journal or diary. Journaling is a good way to measure your progress. You may be surprised to learn that what you write today shows marked improvement over what you wrote three months ago. It is hard to say when healing starts, but when looking back, it is easier to see.

Suggestions

• Remember that your family is not a "bad family" or your marriage a "bad marriage" because difficult problems arise. It would be unusual if your marriage and family did not suffer. Learning to live with the death of a child is one of the most difficult tasks any family can undertake.

• Try to understand that it is rare for any two people to grieve the same way. Pay attention to your own grieving needs and do what feels right for you. Likewise, try to respect the needs of others who live with you.

• Try to keep talking with your mate and with surviving children about how you feel. Attempting to hide your feelings from your family is like covering a cancer with a bandaid. The pain always comes through. You will all be healthier if the pain is out in the open. It is good for you to cry together.

• If your family is unable or unwilling to support you in your grieving, look for a support group of people who understand. Consider the organizations that have been formed to help grieving parents, such as Mothers Against Drunk Driving, Parents of Murdered Children, and Compassionate Friends. Look for a counselor, chaplain, or spiritual leader with skills in helping people who are experiencing grief following trauma.

• Collect as much information as possible about how your child was killed. This information can be obtained from police reports, autopsy reports, and by talking to witnesses. It is important to collect this data for two reasons: Your mind will rest better if you can "make sense" of the experience; and, through collecting data, you can place blame and responsibility appropriately.

• When disagreements and misunderstandings occur in your family, try not to vent anger by yelling, screaming, or verbally attacking one another. Own your anger, but try not to target someone else in your family. Say, "I love you" every time you feel even a hint of love. These words will be cherished.

• If sexual needs differ between you and your mate, talk about it and try to reach a reasonable compromise. Hugs and tenderly holding each other can be lifesavers, even when more explicit sexuality may not be possible.

• Consider keeping a journal or a diary. It can be helpful not only to give you a way to release your feelings, but also to help you measure your progress in getting better.

• Remember that allowing yourself to feel better does not mean that you are forgetting or being disloyal to your child. It means continuing to grieve, but becoming less overwhelmed by it. It means that you believe that life, as it goes on, matters. For your own sake and for others who need and love you, you have a responsibility to try to feel better.

• Have patience. Realize that the traditional "one year of grief" is not enough. Only a combination of time, patience, and effort will lead to resolution of the pain, and you will never be totally free of it. How hard you work at it and how long it takes are up to you.

What I Want to Remember From This Chapter

Chapter Four

DEATH OF A BROTHER OR SISTER

Special bond.
Precious relationship.
Profound loss.
Sister. Brother.
Painful void.
Please understand.
– Jean Lewis

The death of a brother or sister is a crisis for both child and adult siblings. Yet, they are often neglected grievers.

Young siblings are vulnerable to emotional problems that are similar to those of their parents following trauma. Interestingly, though, many children seem to cope better than adults do. Sometimes, because their grieving is intermittent, adults think they are coping better than they actually are. Much of what we understand about adult grieving is also true for children:

> • A sudden violent death requires different coping skills than an anticipated non-violent death.

> • If a child has emotional difficulties before the death of a sibling, and/or if the family suffers marital discord, the child may be more vulnerable to long-term effects of the trauma.

> • If a child's brother or sister is killed at a time when

their relationship was troubled, guilt can make the death more difficult.

• If a child has emotional support from the parent(s) or a major caretaker after the death, and is encouraged to express his or her feelings, the child usually will adjust satisfactorily.

If you are a parent whose child has been killed, you are probably finding yourself needed by too many people. You attempt to comfort your mate, relatives, and friends because they can't come to grips with what has happened to your family. At some point, their needs can overwhelm you, and you must withdraw to survive.

You may be tempted to withdraw from your children by putting them on a plane or bus and sending them off to be with someone else who loves them. You wish you could help them escape the pain, and you feel guilty because you cannot comfort them. Simply "hanging on" yourself may be your top priority or the only task you can handle.

It is best for families to stay together and grieve together after a sudden death. A young child should not witness the total collapse of a parent, but tears that overflow from sadness for what has happened should be shared. It is impossible to go through life without hurting. It would be wonderful if we could promise our children life without pain. We can't. Grieving together will teach your child that ugly and unfair things happen, and that all of you can survive them.

Young children look to their parents as models. They also believe, at least until they reach adolescence, that parents are all-powerful and all-knowing. They trust you more than ever if you are honest about your feelings and if you do not tell them half-truths about what happened. A child who watches a lot of television or sees a lot of movies may have warped ideas about death. Therefore, honest communication can result in valuable lessons for your child.

Like adults, children differ in the ways they react to death. Age, ethnic customs, religious beliefs, and the relationships they had with the sibling before death all factor in to how they react. How the parents react to the death, however, is the greatest determining factor in how the surviving children react.

Children are not miniature adults, however. Children have their own distinct ways of understanding things. Much of that is determined by how old they are.

Young children differ from adults in that they can endure strong feelings for only a short period of time. As an adult, you may feel that your grief goes on and on. A few years from now, you will look back and see that you are better than you were before, but now it may seem that the pain is constant.

A child, on the other hand, grieves deeply for awhile, and then seems to be content and carefree. Behavior varies widely from hour to hour. One minute the child may be acting out in a violent burst of anger. The next minute, he may want to play games.

Children grieve on an intermittent basis for years after the death of a brother or sister. As they move through their development levels, they understand death in new ways, and grief returns according to their new level of understanding and emotional maturity. Developmental levels vary greatly in children, as do their environments. Therefore, a child's specific age is not always a clear indicator of how she will grieve. The age ranges below should be interpreted very liberally.

Infants And Toddlers

Before the age of three months or so, a baby may be as content with other caretakers as he is with his mother, unless the mother is nursing. He has little, if any, memory of family members when they are out of sight. If a constant caretaker continues to nurture and care for him, he will react only minimally to a loss in the family.

As the infant grows, he usually develops anxiety around strangers, a sign that he has bonded to his mother or another major caretaker. From that age on, a child who loses a parent will grieve. He clearly knows the parent and depends on the parent to feed, clothe, bathe, communicate, and play with him. His grief after the loss of a parent may look like a diffused sense of distress. He may exhibit whimpering, loss of appetite, loss of speech if he has learned to talk, and finally, quiet resignation. A toddler is not likely, however, to deeply grieve the loss of a brother or sister unless the sibling has assumed a major care-taking role.

A toddler absorbs the emotional reactions within the home, however. Therefore, calm nurturing attention is important. Explanations about death won't have meaning for him. What the people who love him do is more important than what they say. Holding, cuddling, and stroking him are ways of assuring him that he will be cared for. They are more important than words.

Ages Four Through Six

A child in this age range is still unable to understand what death is or that it is permanent. It is likely, though, that he or she had discovered dead birds in the yard or has seen something dead that was simply picked up and discarded. A young child may respond to the death of a sibling, therefore, in a somewhat matter of fact manner. He may speak of the death of his sibling almost as he would the death of a pet. He may be aware that something bad has happened, but not that it is devastating. This can be very upsetting to parents who do not understand that his response is normal for his level of development.

The death of a brother or sister is best explained to a young child in physical terms, because his thinking is very concrete: "Your brother was in his car when another car crashed into it. The other car hit so hard that his body got crushed inside the car. It was broken so badly that his heart stopped working and no one could get it to start up again. Therefore, your brother is not breathing anymore. He can't talk or move anymore. He doesn't have feelings. He can't feel hot or cold, or wet or dry. The part of him that is still here doesn't feel happy or sad. His body doesn't feel anything anymore, so we will bury his body in the ground (or your family's choice for final resting place of the body)."

A child this age will have difficulty understanding the concept of soul or spirit. If you believe in a spiritual afterlife, it is still important to explain to your child that his brother or sister's body will be buried or cremated. You might explain that the part that now lives on is the part that was able to love and have feelings.

If your child is told that his brother or sister has "gone to heaven and is now happy with God," but he sees that the family is extremely sad, he may be confused. If he later learns that his sibling is at a funeral home or a cemetery, he may feel betrayed.

Your child aged four through six has a sense of right and wrong, not so much because of an inner sense of morality, but because he has been praised for doing "good" things and disciplined for doing "bad" things. He still clings to many mystical beliefs based on stories he hears and television shows he watches. Therefore, it is quite easy for him to believe that his brother or sister died because he did something bad. If he has wished his sibling would go away, as all brothers and sisters sometimes do, he may be convinced this wish was responsible for the death. Most children have death wishes. Your family has been invaded by death. Your child may assume, therefore, that it was his fault.

It is extremely important for your child to know that the death of his brother or sister was not his fault. Explaining death in concrete, physical terms will be helpful to him.

Because your young child's vocabulary is still limited, especially when trying to describe feelings, he is likely to try to master his loss through play. You can be supportive to your child if you pay attention to his play, whether it be re-enacting the death, playing funeral, or playing "house." Questions such as, "How does the little brother feel?" can help your child begin to verbalize what he, himself, feels.

At this age, it is fairly natural for your child to develop eating or sleeping problems. In fact, you can almost expect sleeping problems if your child has heard that his bother or sister "died in their sleep" or that dying is "just like going to sleep."

Bowel or bladder control problems can also return and are common symptoms of emotional stress. Consult your doctor if the problems are intense or last so long that you feel they are interfering with your child's health.

Ages Seven Through Eleven

Somewhere in this age range, your child will come to the understanding that death is final and that everyone dies eventually. This awareness can be traumatic because the child is still so dependent on his family that he can't imagine surviving without them. He may realize that he, too, will die. This new awareness is frightening for any child. When his brother or sister, who may be near his own age, died, he faced death intimately, even though he may have never thought about it before. He now realizes children, not just old people, can die.

"My big brother, Joshua Erik Jones, 9 years old, got

hit by a car July 8th. I feel very VERY SAD. I am very VERY MAD at the man who killed my brother! He was really very very drunk. He does not have to stay in jail very long. And I am mad about that too. That man was very very bad. I hope Josh is learning a lot up with God. I don't like to sleep in my bed without Josh in the bedroom. I miss Josh very very much. I loved Josh very very much. The end."

– Jessica Jones, Age 7

For children this age, death is seen as an attacker who intrudes and takes life. Your child may be fearful that he, too, will die. It is a realistic fear, based on what has happened. It would not be unusual for your child to develop fears or phobias about anything related to death. He may complain of physical ailments, withdraw, and become excessively careful and cautious. Some act out behaviorally, becoming more aggressive than before.

If your child is in this age range, he has had more years to experience sibling rivalry, more memories of fights with his brother or sister, and more death wishes than younger siblings.

Even more than when he was younger, he may feel that he was responsible for the death of his brother or sister. He is not intellectually mature enough to persuade himself of his innocence, so he will need help in correctly assessing blame. As you will recall from previous chapters, parents also struggle with tremendous guilt when a child in the family has been killed.

The child in this age range now has an expansive vocabulary and can think abstractly enough to openly express his pain, fears, anger, and guilt. He is not only sensitive to his own feelings, but he can also enter into the feelings of others. He is able to empathize. He not only needs comfort and support, but he can be a source of comfort and support to others. Doing so will make him feel better. He must never be led to believe, though, that he is responsible for making the family feel better. He is not a parent. He is still a child.

It is important that your child participate fully in the family's grieving. He should be told the truth. If he has never attended a funeral, he should be told exactly what to expect. He should share in decisions about the funeral and in grieving rituals during the months and years following. He should be encouraged to be open in his grieving. Very importantly, you should not hide your grieving from him.

Witnessing your grief, your child may attempt to replace his deceased brother or sister as a means of helping you cope. You must tell him clearly that no one can replace the child who died, just as no one could ever replace him in your heart.

Avoid putting the deceased child on a pedestal. It is important for you to remember the child who died as realistically as possible. Because of the guilt concerning the bad times, it is easy to push those times out of consciousness and recall your child as nearly perfect. This can be devastating for siblings. To them, it appears that you love them less and that they can never measure up to what they hear you expressing about your dead child. This can cause them to withdraw now or later when they reach adolescence.

A child in this age range may have difficulty in school. Grieving children are confused and have difficulty concentrating, much like their parents. Chronic school problems may be signs of deeper underlying stress. Professional attention should be sought.

Adolescent Siblings

The developmental goal of adolescence is to "leave home" by separating emotionally at first and then physically. In the process of preparing to separate, your child becomes less family oriented and more oriented toward her peers. She finds out who she is and what she believes by venturing out into unknown territory.

She is insecure and may be somewhat self-centered in order to compensate. She is suffering many losses as she moves through adolescence: the loss of security of having mother and father make decisions for her, the loss of her innocence, and the loss of protections by her family.

Because your adolescent is shaky and insecure, the sudden death of a brother or sister is something she definitely does not want to face. She knows she must, but she may frantically try to escape the inevitable. She faces several dilemmas. She is mature enough to understand life like an adult. However, she is more vulnerable than many adults because she is experiencing so many other losses and changes.

A teenager has the capacity for empathy, but because she is ultimately self-centered, as she has to be in order to become "her own person," she may believe that no one has ever felt the deep and powerful feelings that she is now experiencing. Indeed, most adolescents have not experienced anything as devastating as the death of a brother or sister. While a teen needs to lean on her parents for support, she may be reluctant to let these deep emotions show because she is afraid she will seem child-like again.

> "Our three boys were hit by a drunk driver. Dennis and Tim were killed instantly. Jeff survived. It's been six months, and our 16-year-old daughter, Pam, still cannot talk about the boys. My husband and Jeff rarely do."
> – *Ilene Hammon*

The adolescent may be struggling with the same issues as the younger child, including guilt over sibling rivalry if she recently had open conflict with the brother or sister who died. She may think she should take care of her parents who are devastated, or even try to take the place of the dead sibling. As bereaved parents, you may be inclined to turn to your surviving adolescent child for emotional support. Such an expectation, if constant, can be overwhelming. It can also impede your adolescent from "growing up," pulling away from family and becoming more intimate with peers.

An additional source of stress for the surviving adolescent sibling is over-protection from parents. It is almost impossible for a parent whose child has been killed not to have great anxiety when the surviving adolescent is out with friends. This over-protection feels stifling and smothering to teenagers.

All of these pressures coming together for the surviving adolescent can cause her to become self-destructive and engage in alcohol or other drug abuse, to run away from home, or to take risks such as playing "chicken" in an automobile. Flirting with death, so to speak, can be an attempt to gain control. It can also be an escape. Moving fast, keeping the music loud, and forfeiting reality by using drugs are choices she can make to escape the pain.

As parents of an adolescent who has lost a brother or sister, try to be honest and provide emotional support, but do not be surprised if she needs to escape. Doing so, to some degree, is part of normal adolescent development. It becomes even more understandable when the home is filled with so much pain, and she is frightened by her own feelings.

Your adolescent may talk more to her friends about her brother or sister's death than she does to you. She may respond better to another adult who is willing to listen because she does not have to worry about her pain hurting that person as much as it hurts you. You should not be discouraged if she reaches out to someone other than you. That is normal for her stage of development.

Adult Siblings

Most people fail to recognize how deeply adult siblings grieve. If your sibling was older, you shared life with him or her since you were born. Even if your sibling was younger, you may not be able to remember life without him or her.

A sibling relationship carries with it a bond that preference cannot sever. When your sibling died, you not only lost someone you loved, but you lost that person's role within the family. If your sibling organized family parties and holiday dinners, someone else must now take on that role. If your brother was the peacemaker during family quarrels, someone must now absorb that responsibility. It is normal that you and other siblings will try to "fill in" some of these roles. Some changes may take place quite naturally and easily, while others feel awkward and can create conflict within the family.

Part of your role within the family may be related to birth order. If your oldest sibling died, you may have lost a caregiver or someone to whom you've always looked up. If the "baby" of the family died, you may have lost the one you protected the most. If the age difference was great enough between you and the brother or sister who died, you may feel almost as though you lost a parent or a child.

When a brother or sister dies, you also experience a gap in birth order. If the oldest sibling was killed, the second oldest is now the oldest. If there were just two of you, you are now an only child. If the sibling killed was your twin or part of a multiple birth, you may be feeling that part of you died, too. You will need to work hard at rational thinking to prevent yourself from concluding that the wrong one died.

Many bereaved siblings find it difficult to answer social questions. When someone casually asks, "How many brothers and sisters do you have?" or "How many are in your family?" you may feel unable to respond. There is no "right" way to answer these questions, and you may answer differently from time to time depending on how you feel and the setting in which you find yourself.

Assuming that you had three brothers and one was killed, you may want to say, "I have three brothers; two are living, one was killed." You may want to say, "I have three brothers," and leave it at that. On the other hand, you may want to say, "I have two brothers." You have the right to answer these questions in any way you feel comfortable. You can answer differently depending on the setting and whether or not you feel like talking more about it.

For some bereaved siblings, the fact that their sibling's death has altered their relationship with their parents is deeply painful. Chances are, under the stress of coping with the death of their child, your parents will react to you in some ways as though you were still a small child. They are struggling with the senselessness and the unnatural order of being predeceased by one of their children.

You may find your parents attempting to comfort you at the expense of themselves, or trying to protect you from the reality of the death. They may be terrified that another family member may die and may go to great lengths to monitor your activities. If this behavior creates a barrier within the family, talk with your parents and offer them some concrete ways that they can be supportive of you. In turn, invite them to tell you what you could do to comfort them. In times of crisis, it is very easy to fall into old parent/child habits, but it does not have to be that way. They will need to give a little, but so will you.

Similarly, you may find yourself falling into old patterns of behavior in an effort to protect your parents. You may feel that they hurt enough without having to watch you grieve. You may go to incredible lengths to hide your pain from them. It may seem right for you to make decisions for your parents or take on parental responsibilities in an effort to care for them. You may end up "parenting you parents." Usually, though, adult children and parents care for one another because it gives them something to do with their grief. Ask if your parents feel you are over-protecting or smothering them. Respect their response and accommodate as best you can.

In some ways, you may feel as though, in addition to the loss of your sibling, you have lost your parents. Your parents may always have been strong and available for you in times of crisis. Even if you aren't very close to your parents, it can be incredibly painful to become aware of their vulnerability and weakness. This may be the first time you've turned to your parents for support and they can't solve the problem and make it better for you. You may need to grieve the loss of your parents, the parents that were always strong, always in control, never vulnerable.

Ultimately, you will likely forge a new relationship with your parents. Talk with them about what you observe and ask them to share with you how they see you differently. Tell them you want to use these new understandings to build a new, more mature, relationship with them.

Like watching a rock tossed into the lake, you may experience other losses connected with your sibling's death. If your brother or sister married, your family may lose contact with the husband or wife, and with the children. If you want to stay close with them, you may have to be direct about your desires and take the responsibility for staying in touch. Eventually most widows and widowers remarry, which can be a source of hurt to the family of the dead husband or wife. Remember, if you can, that no one will replace your brother or sister, and remarrying isn't an act of disloyalty. A new spouse will probably feel very uncertain about his or her relationship with your family, and will welcome some clarification from you.

If your sibling had children, they are precious reminders of your brother and sister. Discovering traits and physical features in nieces and nephews that are similar to those of your brother or sister is both joyful and painful. Similarly, the special moments in their lives, graduation, marriage, the birth of a child, will be bittersweet as they will always highlight your sibling's absence. Children, especially those who were small when their parent died, will want to learn about that parent from you and others. Maintaining a relationship with nieces and nephews is one way some bereaved siblings have found to honor the memory of their brother or sister.

If you are married, your own spouse may feel like one of the forgotten survivors. Your spouse may have had a very special relationship with your sister or brother, yet he or she does not have the same official ties with your family. Don't forget to include your spouse and the spouses of other brothers and sisters in family events following the death of your sibling. They have also lost the person you were before your brother or sister was killed. While their grief may be different, it must be recognized and accepted just as is yours.

Suggestions

- Be careful about explaining death in half-truths to younger children who need honest, concrete explanations of what has happened. If the child hears, "Your sister has gone away for a very long time," he may feel that his sister has deserted him. He may interpret the desertion as punishment and develop strong feelings of guilt. "Your brother has gone to heaven, is, in itself, impossible for a young child to understand, especially when he learns that the body is buried in the cemetery. The statement, "Dying is like going to sleep," can frighten a child and can result in fear of going to bed or taking a nap. "Your sister went to the hospital and died," can cause a young child to conclude that hospitals make people die. "Your brother died because he got sick," may cause a child to become fearful of any kind of illness.

• Spend time in play with the younger child who may not have adequate communication skills to talk about feelings and reactions.

• Help your child express his feelings by being willing to express yours. Ask your child questions. If he is reluctant, phrase questions as if they were someone else's. "What would you say to Jimmy if he asked you what happened to your brother?"

• Remember that most children grieve intermittently rather than chronically. Therefore, do not be upset because your child has periods when the death of his brother or sister seems unimportant.

• Children may find it easier than parents to discard personal possessions of the deceased. They may also find it easier to "put their grief aside" and find normalcy in school or play. Remember that your deceased child's friends may be pleased to be given something that belonged to your child.

• Protect young children from witnessing an emotional collapse, but otherwise share your grieving with them so they learn that families can survive very painful experiences.

• During the early days of grieving, it is helpful for children to have a personal "ally" to provide stability and understanding. This person calms the anxious child and relieves the parents of total responsibility.

• Siblings aged six, seven, or older should be given all the facts about their brother's or sister's death as they become known. Not being told the truth only enhances a growing sense of being unimportant in the family.

• If you see another child who reminds you of your child who died, point this out to the siblings and explain the grief spasm it has caused. Mysterious behavior on the part of the parent enhances the sibling's fear of being left out or of not being loved as much as the deceased child.

• Even though you share your grief with your surviving children, do not depend on them to take care of you emotionally. Recognize that adolescent children may not want to grieve with you. Do not ask surviving siblings to "be strong" for you or for anyone else. That is too great a burden to carry.

• Talk with surviving brothers and sisters about pleasant memories of the child who died as well as unpleasant memories. This will help them to understand that the child who died was not perfect. Placing the dead child on a pedestal can cause great insecurity for surviving siblings.

• Try not to feel threatened if adolescent siblings seek out other adults or peers for support. That is normal for their developmental level.

• As an adult sibling, spend some time focusing on the role of your brother and sister in the family and how you can enable sensitive and meaningful role transitions within the family. Be gentle with yourself and with your parents.

What I Want to Remember from This Chapter

Chapter Five

DEATH OF A MATE, PARTNER, OR LOVER

The sudden or violent death of a husband, wife, partner, or lover is among the most stressful of losses. No matter what your age, you are not ready to be suddenly abandoned by the person you depended on the most.

You can find many books that address the death of a spouse in your local bookstore, but most of them address death following illness. This chapter focuses on aspects of grieving that relate to sudden death.

Roles and Responsibilities

Your mate probably fulfilled many roles in your household and in your life. Your mate was co-manager of your home and, in many cases, co-parent or step-co-parent of your children. Together you decided how to spend money, make career decisions, discipline children, and entertain friends. Your mate or partner may have been your best friend.

If you and your mate shared most of these roles, you may be left feeling overwhelmed by the fact that you are now fully responsible for them.

Couples divide responsibilities in many different ways. Some choose to separate responsibilities rather than share them. For example, one partner may pay the bills, maintain the car and yard, decide on major purchases, and do the financial record keeping. The other may be responsible for in-home maintenance, primary care of the children, and entertainment. Following an unanticipated death, the surviving partner must suddenly assume new roles that feel awkward and frustrating. To be forced to learn a number of new roles in the midst of grieving is a monumental task.

You may never have operated a clothes washer or dryer. You may never have planned a weekly menu and shopping list. You may not know how to cook. You may be totally ignorant about automobile maintenance. You may not know how to make repairs around the house. You may not know what records to keep for income tax purposes. You may not understand about certain bank accounts, annuities, investments, or other financial matters for which you are now responsible.

The frustration involved in learning the tasks, one by one, is exaggerated even more if you also now assume sole responsibility for children. The children are grieving, too, and all of you feel abandoned, even if the death was not your partner's choice.

In addition to all of this, your financial security may be threatened. If the deceased partner provided all or part of the household income, you may face a complete change in lifestyle. A later chapter in this book will help you through the first months, but you may eventually need to make major changes in order to be responsible and survive financially.

Sadly, you must also expect changes in the way you are perceived by your friends. If you and your mate shared social relationships with other couples, you may find that you no longer "fit" in the group. If you continue to be included, you may realize that even though you are present, you feel lonely in the group. You may start to feel uncomfortable around other people's mates, fearing your interactions could be misinterpreted. If your social relationships centered on your mate's employment or circle of friends, you may sense that you no longer belong.

The absence of physical intimacy is one of the most difficult aspects of the death of a mate. Sexual interest may wane as you grieve, but most people continue to need touching and holding. These yearnings go unsatisfied until another relationship can be established. Yet, a new relationship may be the last thing on your mind. This attitude can change, depending on your age and the quality of the previous relationship, but right now you don't want to think about it.

Dependence/Independence

To enhance the healing process, it is important to understand dependence/independence issues as you try to endure the death of your mate. It is natural for two people living together to be emotionally dependent on each other. The degree of dependence you placed on your mate may have a major influence on the state of your grieving.

Some couples are wholly dependent on one another. Each one feels only half of a whole. With the death of the other half, they have difficulty imagining they will ever be able to function alone.

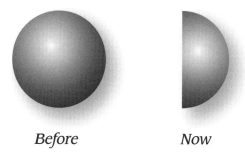

Before   *Now*

Some couples share responsibilities, but experience themselves as independent individuals who rarely "need" each other to feel good about themselves. They love and enjoy each other, but do not lose a sense of themselves when their partner dies.

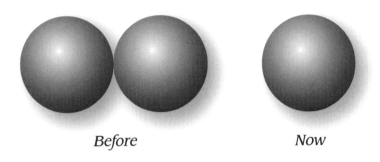

Before   *Now*

Other couples feel primarily independent, but realize that each depends on the other for certain aspects of life. They experience both dependence and independence.

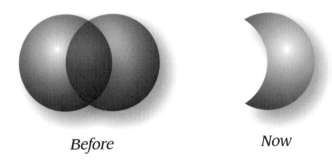

Before   *Now*

Mates with some degree of independence generally will cope with the sudden death of a partner better than those who were excessively dependent. If you were in an emotionally-dependent relationship, you will have the task, eventually, of learning how to be a more independent person. In time, you will shed the image of a "partner's other half" and enhance your sense of individuality, but it will take time and effort.

If you successfully separated from your parents and achieved a sense of independence and autonomy before entering the relationship with your mate or partner, this process may be one of rediscovery. On the other hand, if you were originally dependent on your parents and then became immediately dependent on your mate, you may find it more difficult to adapt to living alone. Rediscovering your own autonomy may require dramatic growth if you decide to work on it at the same time you are grieving the death of your mate. You may find a grief therapist or family counselor helpful if you feel you are getting stuck. Or you might choose to work in a more slow, quiet way, testing your independence daily until you see that you have reoriented and adjusted.

While such growth and adjustment toward autonomy is tedious and painful, most surviving spouses will tell you that it is worth the effort. Learning to endure independently is both challenging and rewarding. Those who achieve it appreciate the fact that they can eventually establish another relationship out of desire rather than need.

What does this kind of growth look like? It means moving from indecisiveness to feeling good about independent decision-making. It means shifting from helplessness to helpfulness. It means replacing intense yearning and sorrow with celebration of what you had, the memory of which you will never lose.

If you were a more independent mate to begin with, your adjustment may not be so difficult. You may not feel helpless and indecisive, but you still may wonder why you feel so anxious and lonely. Some people need to be needed. Parents are always needed when their children are small, and, while sometimes cumbersome, it also feels good. These feelings change as children grow more independent. Perhaps you chose to live with a partner who needed you as much as wanted or desired you. If you liked that and it made you feel important, you may feel unimportant now.

In order to feel better, you might find yourself looking for relationships with dependent people. They feel familiar. If you send out conscious or unconscious signals that you like dependent people, you surely will find them.

You may want to re-evaluate the pros and cons of a dependent relationship. Remember what it felt like for your mate to have been so dependent on you. You may decide that you want future relationships to be different.

Satisfying/Difficult Relationships

All people experience some ambivalence in their relationships. In the most affectionate of relationships, couples still experience anger from time to time, even hostility. However, most relationships are basically satisfying or basically conflict-ridden.

If your relationship with your mate was generally satisfying, mutually rewarding, and if you have few guilt-producing memories, you will probably cope better than those whose relationships were conflict-ridden.

Consider the loss of a satisfying relationship. Looking closely, you may find that although you deeply grieve the death of your mate, you have little about which to feel remorseful or guilty. You have many memories to cherish. You can say that your life together was something to be celebrated.

If your relationship with your mate was conflict-ridden, you might actually feel some relief from the conflict as the shock of the death wears off. However, that relief may be replaced with a remorse you don't understand. Even though the relationship was negative, the feelings and attachment may have been strong. A difficult relationship is still binding.

You may feel guilty because you weren't able to work things out. You may be obsessed with memories you wish you could forget. Even though you know it's impossible, you long for another chance to make your relationship different. Sometimes the guilt is so painful that you unconsciously repress it and actually forget the hostility you previously felt. What you feel becomes, literally, too much to bear.

This is not unlike what children from unhappy homes experience when they are removed from their families and placed in foster homes. Relieved at first to be safe, they eventually forget about the abuse and long to return home. They become convinced that problems in the family were their fault, and they are sure it would be different if they could be reunited with their family.

Wishing for another chance when you know you will not have it can leave you feeling guilty, depressed, anxious, and yearning for your deceased mate. You may decide consciously or unconsciously that remaining stuck in depressive mourning is the only way you can make it up to your dead mate. Intellectually, you know this does not make sense, but the feelings can be difficult to overcome.

Your task in getting better is to recall honestly both the strengths and weaknesses of your relationship. It is appropriate to be remorseful for failures in your relationship that were your fault. It is possible, however, that you will put your dead mate on a pedestal to counter the ill wishes you had toward him or her in life. You may conclude that problems in the relationship were all your fault. Your task will be to evaluate the relationship rationally. Ask yourself what failures in the relationship were your mate's. What things about your mate did you resent? What did you appreciate? How much of the responsibility should be placed on you mate? How much on you? As you answer these questions, you should be able to set aside some of your irrational guilt.

In summary, you are who you are, in part, because of the relationship you had with your mate. You are now changed by your experiences in coming to grips with his or her death.

You probably will never get "completely over" the relationship or the loss of your partner. Your life with your partner has influenced who you are now. Even as you eventually feel ready to begin a new life, you will not forget the past. Your task is to understand the changes that have taken place, accept them, and develop the rest of your life in the face of this new reality.

Suggestions

• Consider the roles and responsibilities that formerly belonged to your mate. Decide which ones you must now assume and which ones are optional. You may want to ask someone else to take over some of the optional responsibilities. You may decide that some can be let go.

• Do not make hasty decisions that involve substantial sums of money. Seek out a trusted friend, relative, or a professional financial advisor to help you make these decisions wisely.

• Make an effort to maintain some social relationships, even if it means discovering new groups or making new friends.

• Acknowledge that you have physical intimacy needs, and look for constructive ways to meet those needs. Some people find massage by a legitimate masseuse to be a practical solution for touch deprivation. Pets that enjoy being stroked can also be comforting. Even taking care of plants can involve you in intimate contact with living things.

• Evaluate the dependence/independence aspects of your previous relationship. If you decide you want to make changes in yourself, now that you are alone, seek out a professional counselor to help you identify and accomplish this goal.

• If your relationship was conflict-ridden, evaluate it realistically. Be objective about placing the responsibility, and do not take more than your share. Identify resentments and appreciation of your mate. Evaluate your own strengths and weaknesses.

• Realize that coming to grips with the death of your mate will take courage, hard work, and patience. Getting better may take more time than you realize. Understand that you are changed by what has happened.

• Don't be so frightened of the pain of grieving that you try to escape it by becoming excessively active, entering into other relationships prematurely, or using large doses of medications, alcohol or other drugs. It is better to lean into the pain and fully experience it as you are able.

• Seek out support groups specifically for persons who have suffered the death of a loved one after a tragic death, or for persons who are widowed. You will gain hope for getting better as you see how others have survived, changed, and are coping.

• Understand that you are likely to face other losses, although they are not likely to be as traumatic as the loss of your partner. Try to be aware of your progress in grieving the death of your mate. Identify tools for coping that may help you in the future.

What I Want to Remember from This Chapter

Chapter Six

DEATH OF A PARENT

Death of a Parent During Adulthood

It is not unusual for an adult's parent to die. Most parents die before their children do. Adult children wonder about when and how their parents will die. They feel a great deal of sadness as they watch their parents becoming forgetful, frail, and slowing down.

Very few adult children, however, consider the possibility that a parent could be killed suddenly. While they may think about things they want to tell their parents before they die, most adult children put them off, or write them in a Mother's Day or Father's Day card. They feel confident that at some time in the future, the time will be right to tell their parents how much they love and appreciate them.

Nothing feels right when a parent is killed or takes his or her own life. Even when the parent is elderly, an adult child can expect the devastation to be as great as that described in previous chapters of this book. Additionally, the killing of a parent presents some unique aspects of grieving.

The longer your parent lived, the more memories you have to cherish. Likewise, the more regrets you have about things you did or did not do.

Many people feel somewhat child-like when visiting their parents, even if they are thirty, forty or fifty years old. Most of us want to share our life's highs and lows with our parents. Even as adults, we want our parents to be proud of us.

A significant part of growing up is "cutting the apron strings," becoming independent, and directing our own lives. Yet even those who are most successful at becoming independent know that at some level, a part of them always remains their parents' child.

Thus, when a parent dies, an adult child can feel suddenly void of nurture and guidance. This can be especially true if the parent's death was sudden. Your partner or mate holds a unique relationship with you that can be a special source of care and nurture. Your child, likewise, loves you in a special way. Yet, after a parent is killed, you may realize that he or she still meant much more to you than you realized. If this death was that of your last parent, becoming suddenly parent-less can leave you with a strange and new sense of insecurity.

Another difficult component of grief after the sudden death of a parent is their loss of dignity. Everyone hopes that their parents will die with dignity. Most hope to be able to say that their parent lived a good, full life, and died peacefully in the presence of loved ones. That seems only fair and just after all the parent gave to the child and others in life.

While the "time" is rarely right for anyone's death, it is even more difficult if your parent died a victim of someone's unnecessary violence or negligence. Even if your parent was in some way negligent or responsible for what happened, it does not seem right that a long life could suddenly be snuffed out in an instant. Being killed is not a dignified way to die.

A third difficult component of grief after the homicide or suicide of a parent is your sudden change in roles. Before your parent died, you were the "middle generation." You had a parent or parents. You may have had a child, or at least anticipated having children some day. Suddenly, in an instant, you are the "older" generation. You may, for the first time, see your children as heirs, as you now become an heir. It is unsettling to think of yourself as the older generation. You do not feel experienced or wise enough to fulfill that role. Thus, even as an adult, you grieve the loss of your own innocence and dependence. No longer having a parent to lean on, you may feel thrust into maturity before you are ready.

How you respond to death depends on many things, including how you have learned to cope with other previous losses, how much emotional support you have as you grieve, and how skillfully you are able to maneuver legal matters such as insurance, wills, or civil and criminal procedures. If your parent did not have a spouse and did not leave a will, you may find yourself in a stressful situation with your siblings about what to do with your parent's property and assets.

Most of all, how you grieve depends on the relationship you had with your parent. The better the relationship, the fewer the regrets and the more minimal the guilt. If you were dependent on your parent, however, you may feel more lost than others. You may experience deep longing for your parent which seems impossible to resolve. In a sense, you might feel too weak to go on without your parent.

You may find your grief experience even more difficult if you had a troubled relationship with your parent. Many children, whether they are young or adult, believe that difficulties with a parent are their fault. Even abused children sometimes spend a lifetime trying to measure up to the expectations of their parents. They believe that one day they will figure out what to do or say that will please the parent and make the parent feel proud of them.

If you and your parent did not get along, you may feel guilty for not trying harder to work it out. You might find yourself full of rage toward the person responsible for your parent's death, because your desire to make things better became futile so abruptly.

If you review your past and realize that you spent a lot of time feeling bad about yourself, those painful self-images can resurface following the death of your parent. If you feel guilty or empty because you somehow link the death of your parent with your bad feelings, you may want to seek professional counseling. Counseling can help you determine the rationality of your thinking.

Most adults whose parent is killed feel some or all of the reactions noted above. It is important to face all your feelings and to give yourself time in solitude to both mourn your loss and to remember the good times you enjoyed with your parent. To do only one and not the other is to abort part of your grieving.

Our hustle-bustle "get over it" society can make it difficult for you to grieve the loss of your parent. More than any other age group, you will be expected to "get on with your life" very soon since it is considered "natural" for adults to lose their parents.

You may be surprised to find that even your best friends fail to ask how you are or to acknowledge your grief. When a child's parent is killed, he or she is called an orphan, and many people are concerned. When a spouse is killed, the surviving partner is called a widow or widower, and friends and neighbors offer help, at least for a while. However, there is no name for the adult child whose parent is killed. People seem to minimize your grief, even when your parent has died a sudden, undignified or unnecessary death.

Death of a Parent During Childhood

Much has been discussed about the traumatic grief of children in Chapter IV. The reactions of children to the death of a parent and the death of a sibling are similar, but differ in some ways, too.

As with siblings, the impact of a parent's death on a child depends much on the child's developmental stage. No one knows for sure why some children cope better than others do. Life experiences tend to make some children more resilient to change than others. However, the quality of care assumed by the surviving parent or subsequent caregiver may be the most important aspect in influencing how a child endures the loss of a parent.

The initial response of most children who understand that death is permanent is fear for their own survival. They cannot imagine anyone other than their parent putting them to bed, getting them up, feeding them, and clothing them. The insecurity of an adult child whose parent was killed has been discussed. For a young child, that sense of vulnerability is even greater.

Additionally, surviving children may fear their own death. If a child's parent can disappear suddenly and without cause, a child thinks, so can he.

Children tend to see their parents as wise and all knowing, especially prior to adolescence. A child whose parent was killed is forced suddenly to face the reality that the parent was not wise enough or strong enough to prevent being killed. If the parent could be killed, the child can, too.

Guilt is a third component commonly present in grieving children. Children know they have angered their parent from time to time. They remember times they resented the parent for disciplining them. They may wonder if their negative thoughts toward the parent were somehow responsible for the death. If a child believes this, he can feel terribly guilty and wonder if he, too, might die.

Trust is believed to be the foundation of a child's emotional development. If a child can trust by experience that he will be fed when hungry, diapered when wet, and nurtured when lonely, he decides, long before he can verbalize it, that life is good, the world is safe, and getting his needs met is predictable. The remainder of his emotional development rests on that foundation.

The sudden death of a parent can shatter that trust, although it doesn't have to. One of the most complex components of adapting to a parent's sudden or violent death is the fact that most or all of the surviving adults in the family are devastated. The remaining spouse, grandparents, aunts and uncles, and other family friends may all be so absorbed in their own reactions that they forget to or can't reach out to the children.

If a child is shuffled from one temporary caretaker to another, he may feel emotionally "out on a limb." He may experience physical neglect and emotional abandonment. He may no longer believe that his needs will be met. Even though he may not fully understand death, it is clear that those who surround him are weak and insecure about what they should do.

Therefore, it is important that a consistent, predictable system of caring for the child be established quickly. This is not a simple task. No one can perform parenting exactly like another. However, if the child knows he can trust someone to feed, clothe, bathe, and love him, he can then participate in grieving with the family. Otherwise, fears for his physical survival, withdrawal, and anger will be primary.

It is equally important for a trusted adult to explain to the child who is old enough to communicate why the parent died. If the cause of death is known, it should be discussed honestly and simply with the child at his level of understanding. The caretaker should tell the truth and answer the child's questions. If it appears that the child feels guilty or is especially fearful and anxious, the child must be made to realize that his parent's death wasn't his fault.

Misunderstandings about these issues can cause a child to be afraid and angry because his life is out of control. However, if he believes that he will be cared for, that the death was not his fault, and that he is not likely to die soon, he will probably endure in a healthy manner.

It must be remembered, though, that as a child matures, he may need to grieve the parent's death repeatedly, based on new developmental understandings. Life changes that are normally stressful for children may be even more difficult for the child whose parent has been killed. Adolescence, re-marriage of the surviving parent, leaving home, and facing deaths of other loved ones can be tumultuous.

Suggestions For Adult Children Whose Parent Was Killed

• Be prepared for the fact that few people, if any, will understand the trauma you experience when your parent is killed.

• Look for ways to honor your parent with the dignity his or her death lacked. Establish a memorial fund or trust to honor your parent. Write a memorial or poem about your parent's life and share it with others.

• If you had a troubled relationship with your parent, write letters to him or her expressing your feelings. Write a letter to yourself from your parent, explaining how you think he or she saw the problem. These letters form a "grief work journal" that can help you adjust and heal. Writing can also help you decide how much guilt is appropriate. If you still find it impossible to be rational about your relationship with your parent, consider professional counseling.

Suggestions For Surviving Spouses or Other Caretakers of Children Whose Parent Has Been Killed

• Maintain a routine for the child that is as stable and consistent as possible.

• Try to ensure that the mode of discipline to which the child is accustomed remains the same.

• If the surviving parent is so preoccupied with his or her own grieving that the child and his needs become an irritant, ask someone to come into the home for several weeks or months to share the parenting load. This is preferable to sending the child away, which can make the child feel even more abandoned and fearful.

• Avoid becoming dependent on the child for your own nurture. While your grieving can be shared and can bring you closer to each other, the child will sense your neediness if you become too dependent. It is too big a load for a child to carry.

• Be alert to persistent fears, anxieties, guilt, or anger. Acting out behaviors such as temper tantrums, clinging, or daydreaming in school or at home may be cries for help. Seek counseling for your child if you feel his problems are beyond your scope of expertise as a parent.

What I Want to Remember From This Chapter

Chapter Seven

DEATH OF A SIGNIFICANT OTHER, FRIEND, OR COLLEAGUE

In this mobile and disconnected society, friends and co-workers are sometimes more intimate with one another than family. You can be transparent with a good friend, taking off your masks and sharing your secrets. You may have told your friend things you couldn't tell your parents or your spouse.

Sometimes, a good friend becomes a lover, and the nature of the relationship dictates that it cannot be openly acknowledged. When a partner in an affair dies suddenly, the other is left alone and isolated, perhaps unable even to attend the funeral. At best, others acknowledge the relationship as only a friendship.

By law, in many states, gay and lesbian partners are considered no more than friends. The emotional turmoil felt when one partner in an unacknowledged relationship dies suddenly can be devastating.

Ex-spouses often remain good friends, particularly if they continue to co-parent their children. Yet, because others perceive that the death of an ex-spouse makes life simpler and happier for the one who survives, few, if any, acknowledge the grief. The former spouse rarely is offered the opportunity to share in planning the funeral because the new spouse is the "legitimate" mourner. The death of an ex-spouse should not simply be glossed over. The former spouse invested significantly in the marriage, even if it dissolved years ago. In spite of all that has transpired, it is painful to learn the details of the death and, if the marriage produced children, to stand by helplessly witnessing their suffering at the death of their parent.

Colleagues at work are often among our closest relationships. We depend on them, reveal our ideas to them, share lunches and breaks with them, and seek their counsel. Sometimes it is only after the death of a fellow worker that we realize that someone formally considered a colleague had become a friend.

Among the most ignored mourners are those whose work environment lends itself to frequent exposure to death. Those involved in police work, hospice care, trauma hospitals, or other settings where death is common, frequently find that their own colleagues, friends, and relatives assume that they have become accustomed or even callused to death. Even when the death is sudden, these silenced mourners are expected to buck up and handle it in the routine manner for which they were trained.

Regardless of the unique description of the relationship, a close, meaningful, and powerful affiliation has become suddenly gone. This relationship may have had the power to change your life or help direct your goals. The person who died may have cared for you unconditionally while objectively confronting you with things you could not see. Those relationships are welcomed in a friend or colleague, even though they might be less readily accepted in a family member.

The point is that the family, the funeral industry, your employer, or the law may not consider you a legitimate mourner. Even if you were closer to the deceased than a brother or sister, you may have sat alone at the funeral. No floral shops rang your doorbell. You were not eligible for bereavement leave at work other than a few hours to attend the funeral.

To some degree, you may find yourself accepting society's label as a disenfranchised mourner. In fact, you may now have assumed the role of supporting the "real" family. You may prepare food and help take care of other material needs for them, if any degree of relationship has been acknowledged.

As you struggle to stifle your mourning at work, you may find your supervisor intolerant of your diminished work production. Because you may be experiencing many or all of the grief symptoms and mourning reactions noted earlier in this book, you are a traumatized person, even though no one seems to notice or care. Indeed, if they do notice, you may be criticized for your reaction. Trauma grief reactions that can affect your work include exhaustion, withdrawal, difficulty concentrating, and irritability. Trauma grief can turn into depression. Fear can turn into anxiety or panic attacks. If you experienced or learned of the death at work, simply walking past the area where the death occurred or where you received the death message can trigger spasms of grief.

If your deceased friend was a work colleague, others may share your grief, even if it is only in the break room. Seek out those who seem to be mourning with you and get together outside the work environment. Share your memories of the one who died, and talk openly about your appreciation and regrets. This acknowledges the reality of what happened and provides the social support you need. It may even be possible to organize a short-term support group at work. Meet together during lunch or for an hour before or after work. Talking about your grief makes it more manageable. Realizing that you are not alone in your grief can relieve some of the burden.

You may decide to ask your supervisor if your colleague's desk can remain vacant for awhile, a tribute to his or her life. You may even want to place flowers or other mementos on your colleague's desk. Some people have filled the desk with snapshots and other photos of the deceased person.

If your deceased friend did not work where you do, you may feel isolated at your job. Your colleagues are not likely to respect your mourning and lack of productivity. You must be honest with them. Explain the nature of the severed relationship to your supervisor. Use words "like a brother or sister" if that is true. While you may not be granted bereavement leave, you may want to take a few days of personal leave to go to the cemetery, write in a journal, or seek professional counseling. A counselor who specializes in trauma grief can be of significant help if you cannot find someone to recognize the depth of your loss.

Regardless of where you go for support, your task is to get a few other people to recognize and validate your experience. Tell them what you need. Ask that they allow you to talk about your friend. Ask them to look at your photos and listen to your poems. Perhaps someone will be willing to visit the cemetery with you.

You can further legitimize your mourning by making a memorial donation in the name of your friend. The receiving organization or charity will acknowledge your gift to the family, which will remind them of your special relationship.

If you have the physical and emotional energy, consider a public event of some kind. After her good friend was shot to death while at work in San Francisco, Kimberly Rowland organized a march against the use of handguns.

> "The project, which received significant media attention, provided a way for me to make a significant statement about the value of our friendship and to do all I could to stop gun violence. I later worked with The Bell Campaign, a grassroots organization that opposed guns. While I believe we made a difference, I know for sure that this work helped me make something good from a terrible tragedy."
>
> – *Kimberly Rowland*

Suggestions

• Identify a short phrase that describes your relationship with your friend or colleague such as "like a brother or sister to me" or "closer to me than any of my relatives" to help others understand the significance of your relationship. Use it often.

• Let the family members of the one who died know how special the relationship was to you. This can be achieved through personal visits or a letter that includes stories and photos about your relationship. Except for clandestine affairs, these offerings are likely to be warmly received.

• Visit the cemetery or use other rituals to help you acknowledge the legitimacy of your relationship.

• While you cannot expect your work environment to provide all the support you need, tell your supervisor about the nature of your relationship and acknowledge your work deficits. If you are unable to work productively, ask for a few days of personal leave.

• If you are unable to find people with whom you can honestly and openly share your mourning, seek out a counselor who specializes in trauma grief.

• Find a way to create something positive from your loss. This may be a donation, publication, memorial, or an activity. Use your own creativity to decide what might best memorialize your relationship.

What I Want to Remember From This Chapter

Chapter Eight

SUICIDE

Following a loved one's suicide, you may feel stunned, moving back and forth between a sense of detachment and agonizing sadness, guilt, anger, and confusion. Your emotional reactions may be more intense than you would have thought possible. Almost everyone is perplexed, bewildered, and overwhelmed when confronted with suicide. While your response to the suicide may be similar to those whose loved one was killed by another person, it probably differs in several ways.

Like homicide, suicide results in the sudden, irrevocable end of a loved one's life. You may long to say, "I love you," "I'm sorry," or "Goodbye." If your loved one wrote a suicide note, you may anguish over not being able to respond to it.

Most people don't realize that suicide is as common as it is. According to the Centers for Disease Control (CDC), a person in the United States takes his or her own life every 16 minutes. Suicide is the third leading cause of death for 15 to 25 year-olds (following accidents and homicides). An estimated 5 million United States citizens have attempted to kill themselves. While these facts may slightly normalize what has happened, you are probably more focused, however, on your own powerful and complicated reactions.

Some people kill themselves violently. Others choose overdoses, inhalations, or other less violent forms. How it happened and why it happened might be of great interest to those who attempt to comfort you, but what probably matters the most to you is that a person you loved is no longer alive. In time, you, too, may focus more on the facts, but it is not likely to be your primary concern right now.

Dr. Ted Rynearson was totally consumed with the reenactment of his wife Julie's suicide for weeks after she died. He could not move beyond it to anything else.

> "Once the procession of scenes began to unfold, I could do nothing to interrupt it. It was like a series of spotlighted scenes drawn from one side of my mind to the other. She walks down the ramp to the ferry and sits alone. Now that she has written a note, she doesn't want anyone in her way. When the island becomes a distant margin, she is ready to leave. She walks to the lower deck and through the parked cars to the stern. Drawing her brown, wool coat about her, she jumps into the wake. Merged in this drama, I would imagine what she thought and felt. This imagining was an endless questioning that wouldn't stop. There was no questioning what she had done, but there seemed no limit to my imagining her last thoughts and feelings.
>
> > What went through her mind as stood on the stern of the ferry?
> >
> > Was she saying goodbye to the kids and me before she jumped?
> >
> > Was she welcoming the release of her drowning and the water?
> >
> > What went through her mind after she jumped?
> >
> > Was she frightened by the coldness and suffocation?

Did she scream for help because she realized this was a mistake?

What went through her mind as she died?

Did she feel a calmness and transcendence as she became unconscious?

Was she hoping and searching for awareness beyond her dying?

I kept this experience secret, even though it kept me from maintaining concentration during the day and kept me awake at night. I would awake, crying and terrified as I witnessed Julie disappearing in the wake of the ferry. It would take me hours to calm myself so I could get back to sleep. There seemed to be no time or space for my mind to rest."

— Ted Rynearson, quoted with permission from his book, Retelling Violent Death

Under the extraordinary condition of reliving Julie's suicide, Ted could not differentiate himself from his imaginary story. He saw and heard the reenactment of Julie's dying as if it were not imaginary. In those early weeks after her death, the imagery he developed was so autonomous and powerful that he felt possessed by it. Only later, as he was able to separate himself from it and find his own voice again did he realize that this process had been an important component of how he came to understand Julie's suicide. It was her story. His task then became that of building his own story without her and deciding how to go on.

You may not have become so intertwined in the dying event, but if you are like most suicide survivors, you have a desperate need to understand why your loved one chose to take his or her own life. Perhaps you think that understanding the reason may help you feel less vulnerable and more in control. If you can conclude that it was someone's fault, that someone "missed the signals," or that your loved one had a legitimate reason for the suicide, then it makes some sense. However, there is rarely, if ever, only one reason a person takes his or her own life. Usually, there are many complex reasons.

Since you were close to the suicide victim, you are likely to be inundated with questions from all kinds of people who want the answer to be simple and reasonable. Try to be patient with them. If you don't feel like answering their questions, simply say, "I appreciate your interest. Perhaps one day I can talk about 'how' and 'why,' but right now I'm just sad and lonely, and that's all I can face right now."

Denial and Confusion

"There must be a mistake. He couldn't have committed suicide. He wouldn't do that to me."
    –Anne Seymour, whose friend committed suicide

The most devastating component of suicide to most people, and the component that makes it so difficult to accept, is that it was their loved one's choice to die. It may seem impossible to you that the person who took his or her life was so miserable or felt so unloved that suicide was seen as the only reasonable escape from pain. Confusion and bewilderment may envelop you as you struggle with this reality. Just remember that you will never be able to know all the factors that contributed to your loved one's choice and, for that reason, try not to put too much blame on yourself.

It can even be somewhat comforting to realize that the suicide was a choice. You may find solace in the fact that the victim remained "in charge" and clearly chose to end life. If your loved one was in physical or mental torment, the choice to take his or her life may have been a relief. Since no two suicides are alike, and no two responses to it are alike, only you can decide if any element of relief exists for you. If others feel that you should be relieved and you are not, just tell them that only you can decide how you will react to it.

Anger

> "I'm so mad at him that I could kill him! I'm angrier than I was with the drunk driver who killed my godchild, because that guy was a stranger."
> – *Anne Seymour*

It is not likely that your loved one committed suicide to hurt you or to get even, although that is sometimes the case. He or she probably committed suicide to escape torment so overwhelming that it is impossible for most of us to imagine. The person may have been so consumed by his own sense of overwhelming physical, emotional, and spiritual pain that he felt there could be no relief other than to end his life. Or, perhaps the person was withdrawn and depressed, and developed tunnel vision. Life's problems may have seemed much greater than they really were, and the victim became so focused on them than he couldn't see beyond them to how those who loved him would react to this death.

Sometimes, suicide is manipulative. If you sense that it was committed in an attempt to prove something, it may have been manipulative, and, therefore, your anger about it may be ferocious. Did she mistakenly think that she was unloved? Did she do this to upset you? Did she think that she was too weak to endure a disappointment? Couldn't she see how painfully unfair this would be to you? Didn't she think about the hurt and havoc you would suffer in trying to pick up the pieces? The questions go round and round in your head.

You may be angry with yourself as well. You may torture yourself by ruminating over missed signals or your perception that you failed to take the signals seriously enough. You may have thought of yourself as an aware, caring person, but now feel ashamed and degraded that you allowed this to happen. You conclude that you didn't know your loved one as well as you thought you did. How you felt about this person and how she or he thought about you may now seem called to question. Your self-esteem may take a tumble.

You may also find yourself angry with others who seem to blame you. Remember that people less close to the victim than you are looking for answers. Often, an initial hypothesis is that you were not a good parent, spouse, lover, child, or friend. How unfair! You must remember that they are trying to make sense of a senseless act. Without a doubt, even the victim could not have explained exactly why he chose to end his life. Nor should such an explanation be expected of you, no matter how well you knew and loved him.

You will greatly complicate your grieving if you attempt to suppress your anger. It is a reasonable and appropriate response to what has happened. While you may choose not to make other people miserable with your anger, you need to stay in touch with it and express it with someone safe who can accept your feelings. As stated in previous chapters, leaning into your emotional reactions, accepting them, and exploring them will bring relief more quickly than suppressing them.

As time goes on and as you express your anger, you also will be able to assess the situation more realistically. With the help of an accepting friend or a professional counselor, you can weigh the positive and negative attributes of your loved one and better assess your relationship. Evaluate the rationality of your thoughts and work toward discarding irrational beliefs about your role in the suicide. This takes time and hard work. Be patient with yourself.

Guilt

If your loved one tried to reach out to you before the suicide and you weren't available, you may feel overburdened with guilt. You may now be convinced that if only you had been there, the suicide would have been prevented.

You may feel guilty for not having taken the suicide instrument from your loved one, whether it was a gun, rope, pills, or an automobile. If the suicide instrument was something you gave to or purchased for the victim, you may irrationally conclude that the suicide was your fault.

Those who experience some relief because of the suicide may feel guilty for those reactions. Your religious training or ethical beliefs about suicide may make it more difficult to reconcile your sense of relief.

A Survivor's Experience

"I left the hospital like a zombie, with little recollection of how I drove the thirty miles home. The car soon became my 'raging place.' I found I could cry and scream without disturbing anyone else. So I screamed. The vocal noises sounded eerie, like a wounded wild animal. I did not know where they came from or who they belonged to, only that they needed to come out.

Weekly, I drove to the therapist. I passed smiling people and wondered what there was to smile about. The 'if onlys' haunted me. I felt like a rat in a Kubler-Ross laboratory. Trapped in a grief maze with no way out, I bounded from one 'stage' to another and back again. I made monthly pilgrimages with flower tokens to the remote hill where his ashes were scattered. I'd stand on the hill and scream, 'WHY?'

As I sat in the Mental Health waiting room, I could observe other patients and identify with their individual pain. Although I had previously done social work, this was a new chapter in empathy. 'They' were no longer separate from 'me.' It was 'us' – the human condition creating the common denominator.

It was four months before I began to let go. Suddenly, I became aware of what the inside of the therapist's office really looked like. I had never noticed the plants or the furniture and thought they were new.

I came home and put together a brick/rock pathway, and felt good for the first time in months. I remembered from somewhere that depression blocked creativity. My sidewalk looked beautiful to me.

The weekly trips to the therapist lasted nine months. Eventually I saw that screaming 'Why?' on a hilltop made no more sense than a three-year-old throwing a tantrum. Then one night as I was soaking in the tub, I looked up on the bathroom wall and admired a large sampler my daughter had embroidered. I had it framed years ago and thought it quite an accomplishment for a fourteen-year-old. I had read it often. It was the Serenity Prayer: 'God, grant me the serenity to accept the things I cannot change; the courage to change the things I can; and the wisdom to know the difference.'

I mused a moment, 'I wonder what the wisdom to know the difference really means.' Suddenly, it came. It meant the ability to know and accept my own limitations.

As badly as I wanted it, I could not have made a life choice for him. In respect for his dignity, I finally allowed that he alone had made that choice. The choice was a human one. If humans are not perfect, then neither are their choices.

Who am I to judge?
Rest in peace.
All is forgiven—finally."
    – B.H.B

Human beings have an almost innate conviction that they should be able to protect those they love. While it is impossible and irrational, it is difficult to overcome. You cannot assume responsibility for an act that was someone else's choice.

It is likely that little could have been done to dissuade your loved one from taking his own life. If you were not present when your loved one reached out for help, he would have sought out someone else if he truly wanted to stop himself. If warning signals were given, they were probably hidden in ambivalence. If a gun had not been available, a rope or other means would have been sought.

In coming to grips with your guilt, your task is to transfer your focus to rational thinking. Understand that suicide is extremely complex, and the final suicidal act was only the final component of a much greater context of emotional and mental turmoil. Many internal and external forces come together to enable a person to choose to take his or her own life.

Try to determine what proportion of the responsibility may have actually been yours. The extent is apt to be small if it exists at all. Like all human beings, you are not perfect. You will need to find a way to forgive yourself for any contribution that you can rationally claim. As you think back over everything that happened, you will probably discover that you made the best choices you could based on the information available to you at the time. The greatest proportion of responsibility lies with the person who chose to end his or her life.

Stigma

Suicide is little understood by the public. Some people think that only severely mentally or emotionally ill people kill themselves, and that this capacity is inherited. They can conclude, therefore, that as a relative of the victim, you also are unbalanced and a poor risk for friendship.

Other people think that suicide is purely environmental and that you or someone else "drove" your loved one to death. Either of these erroneous conclusions, or others, can cause people to shun you because of the incident itself, your family history, or your personal lifestyle choices.

Suicide is not a disease. It is not an act of immorality. It is not a biological anomaly, although interesting physiological connections between depression and suicide are now being revealed. In most cases, suicide does not represent neurological dysfunction. Almost always, it is a choice made by a person who has lost hope.

In seeking to avoid the stigma, some surviving family members choose to live a lie about the suicide. They tell others that it was an accident or death due to natural causes. While this may be comforting at first, it can greatly complicate grieving. As previously noted, much confusion surrounds the suicide experience. Choosing to lie about it only enhances the confusion. The additional stress of knowing one thing inside and telling a dissonant story on the outside is stress you don't need.

Although it is unfortunate and sad that you face ostracism, it is usually preferable to disguising the truth. Simply stated, people who live lies often get sick. They begin to suffer physical symptoms and become even more depressed. Something within them avoids repeating the lie, and yet they can't bring themselves to tell the truth.

It is far healthier to talk realistically about what happened and to share your personal reactions honestly with trusted friends or family members. This openness may be your best prescription for beginning to feel better. Your faith leader or a professional counselor can help you face it honestly, and it may be wise to pursue this kind of help.

Second Victimizations

As newspaper reporters, medical examiners and coroners, insurance representatives, law enforcement investigators, and lawyers become involved in the suicide, you may feel that your integrity and moral character are being questioned. If you were close to the victim, or if you were due an inheritance or insurance money, you can find yourself a murder suspect or a suspected accomplice to the suicide. At the very time you want to be treated with dignity and respect, you may have to face accusations that can enhance your guilty feelings and reap even more havoc on your self-esteem.

Regardless of your treatment, it is in your best interest to cooperate fully with investigative authorities. Remind yourself that their role is to determine the facts surrounding this sudden death. Most of them have had no education in the dynamics of trauma-related bereavement, and many are uncomfortable facing emotions.

In order to overcome the powerlessness you may feel in working with these people, ask for documentation of their findings. If there is a criminal investigation, get the name and phone number of the investigating officer and call from time to time until the investigation is complete. Ask for a written copy of the completed report. If it is available in your jurisdiction, obtain a copy and, if you see errors, call immediately to discuss them with the investigator.

If an autopsy was performed, ask for a copy of the report. Autopsies often reveal previously unconsidered rationale for the suicide such as bodies racked with pain, disease you were not aware of, or high concentrations of alcohol or other drugs. Not all states require autopsies on suicide victims, so do not expect one to be performed automatically. In an era where AIDS is feared to an almost irrational degree, medical personnel may resist autopsies in cases where a significant amount of blood was lost, especially if the victim was considered a high risk for AIDS.

The media can become an insatiable pest, especially if the victim was well-known in the community and if any mystery surrounds the death. You have the absolute right to refuse to talk with the media, if that is your choice. Rather than responding "No comment," which can add an even more suspicious note to the event, it is usually wiser to give them a one or two-sentence prepared statement. For example, you may want to say, "We are experiencing great grief because of this death and choose to refrain from public comment at this time." A statement like this can also be written out and handed to members of the press. If you choose to do this, simply turn and walk away after the information is given.

If you are bothered by members of the press or find that your boundaries are not being respected, call the news director of the offending television station or the managing editor of a newspaper. The phone numbers are in your telephone directory or on the Internet. State your concerns firmly and in as few words as possible. Be specific and provide names.

The legal implications of a suicide can be extremely complex. Some insurance companies have prematurely classified accidental death or homicides as suicides in order to avoid paying survivor benefits. Heirs may be eager to prove that the victim was unstable if changes in the will were not beneficial to them. Many suicide victims leave holographic (handwritten) wills as their Final Will and Testament or codicils (amendments) to a previously prepared will. Their financial and legal records may be in disarray as a result of their depression and confusion. Various family members may be eager to handle or interpret documents in a manner that is self-serving to them. All of this can be frustrating to those who loved the victim and are grieving. Under these circumstances, it is usually prudent for all involved in the financial or legal affairs of the victim to retain professional legal counsel.

In some cases, a close friend may have been more intimately involved with the suicide victim than family members. Friends sometimes sense the signals of suicide, are recipients of the suicide note, or discover the body. All too often, these friends are excluded from family grieving rituals and find themselves in an adversarial position with the family, especially if they are named as heirs in the will of the deceased. If families can be sensitive to the emotional needs of friends who are equally devastated, they too may find additional support through the common bond of shared grief.

God and Suicide

Some people feel compelled to share their theological beliefs about suicide with you. Your own spirituality may have been shaken by what happened. While spiritual encouragement would be welcomed, it is not always given. You may realize that you want more information and time before deciding what you believe about this weighty issue. You may want to read Chapter 10 on Spirituality for more information on the subject.

In the meantime, it may be helpful for you to know that six cases of suicide are mentioned in the Old Testament of the Bible. Nowhere does the Old Testament or Hebrew Bible forbid suicide. However, many Jewish theologians consider it wrong out of respect for the body as created in the image of God.

Likewise, the New Testament of the Bible does not forbid suicide. In fact, in the early years of the Christian church, it was sometimes considered a form of martyrdom. However, St. Augustine later decreed in the Fourth Century that it was a sin because it precluded the possibility of repentance and violated the Sixth Commandment, "Thou Shalt Not Kill." Thus, the Catholic Church has generally been more negative about suicide than the Protestant branch of Christianity. In Islam, the Qur'an forbids suicide with the exception of a narrow range of circumstances in combat.

Theologians and philosophers have always debated the subject of suicide. Many New Testament theologians point to the forgiving spirit of God as revealed by Jesus. In asking Christians to forgive "seventy times seven" (generally understood as infinity), Jesus reveals the abundantly forgiving nature of God.

You may want to tell people who seem eager to condemn your loved one that you need time to sort out this issue for yourself. In the meantime, if you believe that God is forgiving, it can be helpful for you to say so.

A Word About Surviving Children

Much of what has been written in this book about the response of children to homicide (See Chapter 4) holds true for children struggling to deal with suicide. Children old enough to realize that death is final should be told the truth about what happened. Being lied to feels like being excluded from the family. When the truth comes out on the playground or in the neighborhood, and the child knows he or she is not supposed to know, it can feel like betrayal. Feeling betrayed makes children afraid, confused, angry, and sometimes guilty because they fear the reason they are not being told the truth is because they did something wrong. The reactions of a child to suicide should be heard and addressed, just like those of adults.

Children sometimes believe that they were somehow responsible for the suicidal death, especially if the person who died had been difficult to live with and the child had wished him or her dead (as most children do from time to time). It is extremely important that the children be told all they can understand about the unhappiness and anguish within the person who took his own life so they don't blame themselves. The victim did not choose to end his life because this child was bad. The victim did not choose to end his life because this child was not with him. The victim did not choose to end his life because this child could have prevented it and did not.

Since children model the adults in their lives, especially parents, they will need education and instruction about suicide. The information previously given in this chapter can be shared with children at a developmental language level they can understand. They need to hear time and again that suicide is not a good choice for failures or a way to solve problems. They need to hear and be able to repeat that suicide is not a good way out of disappointment or depression. These things can be overcome.

Repeated Suicides Within a Family

There is a higher incidence of suicide in families that have experienced a previous suicide. Suicide potential is greatest for elderly white males, especially if they are sick or lonely. Social isolation coupled with alcohol or other drug use is another risk factor. Those widowed by suicide are at even greater risk.

Whether this was the first suicide in the family or a repeated event, there are things you can do to prevent it from happening again. Bring your family together often to problem solve. Build bonds of care and support with the attitude that problems are challenges to overcome, not catastrophes to overwhelm. Be sure that everyone is connected to a faith community or other social group where friends can be leaned on for support.

Don't allow a depressed person to withdraw and isolate. They prefer isolating themselves because relating is too draining. Even if they don't feel like responding, it is important for you, or someone, to be present and to talk, even if the person doesn't respond much. Try to engage in conversation from time to time. Use children and pets to make contact and motivate relationship. Most people who feel bad enough to consider killing themselves still have a part of themselves that wants to find hope and a reason to live. Do your best to provide that.

Watch for what may look like improvement. Most people who kill themselves actually feel better after resolving to do it and exhibit a lift from the previous despair. They may now have found the energy to actually do it. Explore specifics of what the person is doing to feel better and for descriptions of what is planned for the following night or day. Watch for tunnel-vision, in which no way out of psychological pain can be seen. That is the hallmark sign of suicide.

For Michael

Dear Michael with the dancing eyes,
We wonder how your eyes got so blue;
How it was that you were such a handsome lad;
Why it was that you could always make us laugh.

We don't know.

We wonder why you found such delight as a little boy
In decorating the kitchen floor with soap
    Or flour or spaghetti
    Or covering the walls with lipsticks
    Or filling our hearts with joy.

We don't know.

We wonder where you got the drive to hit the homerun,
The flair to tell the funniest joke,
The talent to become a fine carpenter,
The compassion to love your little daughters so.

We don't know.

We wonder about the pain in your heart,
If your romance with death began when your brother
    was killed,
If death was your solution of choice to ease the torment,
If this was your final act of taking responsibility.

We don't know.

We don't know why.
We will never know why.
We don't have to know why.

We don't like it.
We don't have to like it.
We will never be the same.

But we do have a choice about what we do with it.
Let us not ponder on the road not traveled.
Let us not become destroyed and, thus, destroy.
Let us not try to explain the chaos of our world.

Instead, let us remember
        that memories survive,
        that goodness lives,
        and that love is immortal.
        – *Janice Harris Lord, with gratitude to Beckie*
            Brown and Iris Bolton

Suggestions

• Focus on your emotional reaction rather than on the "why" and "how." Understand that it is normal for you to grieve deeply and to feel confused about what has happened.

• Recognize that it is natural for you to be angry with the victim, with yourself, and with others in the aftermath of suicide.

• If guilt becomes a problem, immerse yourself in the facts. Obtain copies of reports. Talk with witnesses, family members, and friends. This will help you gain control and own only the portion of the blame that is reasonable. Realize that you will never discover all the answers.

• Don't let people tell you how you should feel. Your feelings are your own.

• Understand that you may be ostracized in the aftermath of suicide, and that there is little you can do about it except talk openly and honestly about what happened.

• If you are involved legally or financially, retain counsel.

• Remember that your loved one made the decision to take his or her life.

What I Want to Remember From This chapter

Chapter Nine

HOLIDAYS

"We were driving home Thanksgiving and I was thinking about Christmas and how hard it would be. I knew we needed to get it out of our systems and cry, and then try to have a good time. So, for Christmas I gave my parents a picture of Kurt and a little poem called, 'If I Were Here, All I'd Say is I Love You.' We all had a good cry. This Christmas was a little easier.

A friend sends me flowers on Kurt's birthday. It's nice to know that someone remembers and isn't afraid to remember with me.

The YMCA basketball program has a memorial for Kurt. I remember a card from one of his friends who had moved away. The card said, 'Kurt, it is hard for us with you gone. We love you.' Remembering is important. You still need to celebrate what their lives meant to you, even as you celebrate your own life."
– Kim Keyes, whose son, Kurt, was
killed by a drunk driver

Many struggle with the cloud of sadness that surrounds the holidays when the family has experienced a tragedy such as sudden violent death. The onslaught of holiday cheer may seem too much to bear because it can be a cruel reminder of how your family differs from those happy ones in the magazines and on the television commercials. Spring can be difficult because it brings Passover and

Easter, Mothers Day, and Fathers Day, all days to remember the joy of new life. Friends, and even family members, may seem to avoid you during the holidays because they can't face you and your loss, preferring to focus on their own joys.

One mother said, "It seems like everyone is afraid to mention my child's name, probably because they think it will upset me. They need to understand that I will never forget, whether they mention him or not. I desperately need a way to make my child's memory a part of the holiday season. It is senseless to think that I could forget, especially at this time of year."

Groups like Mothers Against Drunk Driving (MADD) set aside a special time during the Thanksgiving/Christmas holidays to remember their loved ones and to express hope for a less violent future. MADD conducts Candlelight Vigils throughout the nation in early December. They are simple with some music and a few brief statements. The most significant feature of this annual ritual is when families come forward to light a candle in remembrance of their loved one. Tears flow, but as one father says, "It's the loveliest way I know to say Merry Christmas and to acknowledge the joy that Janie brought to us for the seven holiday seasons we were all together."

MADD then follows its Vigils of Remembrance with numerous programs to prevent drunk driving during the holidays. Red ribbons on cars remind travelers not to drink and drive. Other programs like safe-rides programs, designated drivers, and media campaigns are highlighted.

Failure to make something positive out of the holidays may give rise to new or returning bouts of depression, panic attacks, and other forms of anxiety for those whose lives have been affected.

Victims of crime and their loved ones often re-experience these life-changing traumas through flashbacks, nightmares, and overwhelming sadness. Some have trouble sleeping, while others don't want to get out of bed. Tears come easily, often when least expected. Old ailments, including headaches, gastro-intestinal problems, and aches and pain may return.

Families who have made this difficult journey offer the following suggestions to help those who may be just starting down this path. Many were surprised to discover that the anticipation of a holiday is more difficult than the actual holiday. Holidays can be manageable if you take charge of the season rather than letting it take charge of you.

Change Traditions

Trying to make this holiday seem like the one before it will only magnify the difference. Gather the family together early and decide which traditions you want to keep and which ones you want to let go. Change holiday plans to accommodate the needs and wishes of those who are hurting the most.

Create a Special Tribute

Some families light a special candle and place it on a holiday table to honor the memory of a loved one who has died. Others keep a chair empty and place a flower or other memorial on the seat. Some write treasured remembrances and place them on a special plate or bowl for those who wish to read them.

Consider Where to Spend the Holidays

Many people think going away will make the holidays easier. This may be helpful if you are traveling to a place where you will feel loved and nurtured. However, if travel is arranged as a means of trying to avoid the holiday atmosphere, remember that American holidays are celebrated throughout this country and in many parts of the world. It is impossible to escape holiday reminders.

Balance Solitude with Sociability

Rest and solitude can help renew strength. On the other hand, friends and family can be a wonderful source of support, especially if they accept you as you are and do not tell you how they think you should feel. If you are invited to holiday outings, make an effort to go. Attend musical or other cultural events that lift your spirits. You may surprise yourself by enjoying special outings, even if you feel like crying later.

Relive Fond Memories

Attempting to go through the holiday season as if nothing has happened can be a heavy and unrealistic burden. Think about holiday seasons you have enjoyed in the past and identify memories you want to hold in your heart forever. No one can take those away from you. Celebrate them and be grateful. If feelings of sadness pop up at inappropriate times, such as at work or in a public gathering, try thinking about what you have rather than what you have lost. Focus on the blessing of the memories in your heart.

Set Aside Some "Letting Go" Time

Schedule time to be alone and release sad and lonely pent-up feelings. You may want to cry or write about your thoughts and feelings. You may want to write a letter to say "goodbye," "I love you," or "I'm sorry." Even though it may feel strange, allow your loved one to write back to you through your pen. You may be surprised at what you write. By setting aside special times to allow painful feelings to surface, it becomes easier to postpone expressing them in public.

Counter the Conspiracy of Silence

Family members may consciously or unconsciously conspire to avoid mentioning the person who died. This is usually a well-intentioned but misguided attempt to protect your feelings. If this seems to be happening, take the initiative by mentioning your loved one by name. This will alert the family that it is important to you to remember your loved one in a special way at this time, and that doing so will not devastate you. Talk with your family about the importance of talking openly about what has happened.

Try to Focus on the Positive

Some people conclude that facing the holidays is simply "awful." By deciding prematurely that "everything about life is awful," you are generalizing irrationally from your personal tragedy. Although you may have difficult times during the holidays, you also may experience some joy. Accept the love and care of others. Reach out to someone else who is suffering. Give yourself permission to feel sad and to experience joy.

Find a Creative Outlet

If you have difficulty talking about your feelings, look for a creative way to express yourself. Write a poem or story that you can share with others. Buy watercolors or oils and put your feelings on paper or canvas, even if it's only splashes of color. Contribute to a favorite charity or organization.

Remember the Children

Listen to them. Celebrate them. Children may have deep feelings that can be overlooked if you spend all your time focusing on yourself. Putting up holiday decorations can be a draining emotional experience, but recognize the significance of these items to children.

A friend or relative likely will be happy to help you decorate or purchase and wrap gifts. Consider shopping online as an alternative to the frenzy of mall shopping, but don't try to "buy" your way out of sad feelings.

Protect Your Health

Physical and emotional stress changes the chemical balance in your system and can make you ill. Eat healthy food and avoid over-indulging in sweets. Drink plenty of water, even if you don't feel thirsty. Take a good multi-vitamin. Get seven to eight hours of sleep each night. Talk with your doctor about an antidepressant or anti-anxiety medication if you think it will help. If you are unsure about how the medication will affect you, talk to your doctor about your concerns.

Utilize Available Resources

People of faith are encouraged to observe services and rituals offered by their church, synagogue, mosque, or other faith community. Many "veterans of faith" can offer you serenity, a quiet presence, and healing wisdom. You may want to look for a support group of persons who have suffered similar experiences. The Mental Health Association in most communities has a list of these groups. If a group does not exist in your area, establish your own short-term group and focus on getting through the holidays. The most valuable helper usually is someone who shares a common experience or understands something about what you're going through. Spend as much time as possible with the people you love the most.

Most important, remember that you can't change the past, but you can take charge of the present, and shape the future. Total recovery may not be possible, but what you make of your experience is largely up to you.

"Michael's birthday was December 22. He was killed on February 4, so that time is very emotional for us. The first Christmas of my married life was spent in the hospital with my own 'babe.' Now, six years later, we still hurt, but we go on. Each December 22, Mike's brothers have a pizza party in his memory. When he would have been 22, nine of his friends got together and ate 22 pieces of pizza. What a marathon!"

– Rita Chiavacci

"Though I know we will do our share of sniffling and sobbing, I also believe the mere act of paging through our shared scrapbook of memories of my mother will serve as a soothing compress to our spirits. The echo of her honey-rasp laugh will carom off the white walls of my father's apartment and pour from a painting that captures her as an arresting thirty-something woman, on the cusp of marriage and a career.

My mother will be there with us simply because she was too indomitable in life to let the little matter of mortality keep her away from any family gathering – especially Christmas."

– Andrew Marton, the first Christmas
after his mother's death, quoted with
permission from Fort Worth Star–Telegram

What I Want to Remember From This Chapter

Chapter Ten

SPIRITUALITY

"I no longer believe that God is a good God."

"I'll never darken the door of a church again."

"Only my faith in God has enabled me to endure this."

"If one more person tells me that God needed another flower in his garden, I'm going to throw up."

All of these are common spiritual reactions following the killing or suicide of a loved one. Some people say that the experience actually strengthened their faith. Some say it had no effect on their faith. Others say it diminished or destroyed their faith. Many say that their personal faith became stronger, but they felt they could no longer participate in their faith community.

Even if you rarely thought about spirituality before your loved one was killed, you have probably thought about it now. When trying to understand something that is beyond comprehension, we often stretch ourselves into realms previously unexplored.

A minister, priest, rabbi, imam, or other faith leader may have officiated at the funeral of your loved one. You probably received faith-oriented sympathy cards. Friends and relatives may have attempted to comfort you with spiritual references to God. When death comes, like it or not, most Jewish and Christian families deal with God; traditional Native Americans deal with the Great Spirit; Muslims deal with Allah (the Arabic name for God); and Hindus and Buddhists seek inner guidance and consolation. Even proclaimed atheists often ponder transcendence in the aftermath of tragedy. For the remainder of this chapter, however, reference will be to "God" since Judeo-Christianity is the most commonly practiced faith in the United States.

Some people experience God as a personal supporter, a presence bigger than life who gives them strength and peace. They say that their faith in God sustains them as they endure their suffering and helps them keep the tragedy in perspective.

Many survivors are confused and frustrated by God's apparent lack of intervention and protection as the death unfolded, and become angry with God. They believe that they were faithful religious people, and God let them down by allowing their loved one to be killed.

> "'I feel so bad. I just can't comprehend it, it's so horrible,' I wrote three months after John was killed. All I can say is, 'Oh my God, Oh my God.' I feel like I'm going to split into pieces. Why did God let this happen? If there's a God, I hate Him."
> – *Margaret Grogan, whose son was murdered*

The faith of some people remains strong, but they get confused and frustrated with the things people say about God. They wonder why, in the midst of staring death in the face, others talk about "eternal life" or "heaven" as if that should take all the tears away.

Friends, relatives, and even the clergy sometimes say religious things that can hurt more than help. Almost always, these people mean well. They want to help you feel better, but they may not know how. More likely, they may not understand that feeling better is simply not possible for you for some time, and that all you really want is for them to join you in your suffering.

> "I rarely attended church before Adrianne was killed. However, the church I belonged to supported me more than I could possibly have imagined. Sometimes people said insensitive things, but I knew they were trying. I found my basic faith getting stronger. I don't think I could have survived without feeling God was with me."
>
> *– Linda Jones, whose daughter was murdered*

Linda Jones was able to see past the inappropriateness of some of the things said to her and accept their efforts as physical manifestations of their care for her and her family. It is also possible that you might misunderstand what others mean when they talk about God.

It Was God's Will.

This "consolation" may be more hurtful to family members than any other well-intended phrase. A sudden, violent death is absurd. Your loved one didn't deserve it. You don't deserve it. Therefore, for God to have willed it makes no sense.

In your pain, you may cry out, "Why? Why?" even though you understand the concrete cause of the killing. You long for a better explanation, a deeper, more profound reason.

It is paradoxical that the more you long for an answer to the mysterious "why," the more difficult it seems to find answers. The cause of a tragic death is usually someone's choice or negligence. It is a "human being" problem rather than a "God" problem. As long as humans have the freedom to make choices, some will choose to be evil at worst, negligent at best, and the innocent will suffer the consequences.

Into the midst of your turmoil about the "why," a well-meaning person may tell you that the tragedy was God's will. Such a person implies that a mystical reason was responsible for your loved one's death, and only God knows the reason. They imply that the reason is beyond your understanding.

Only you can decide if that reasoning makes sense. If this line of reasoning is not acceptable to you, you will probably feel angry and resentful about the explanation. You may identify with the Jewish leader who, when asked if there was a meaning to the Holocaust, responded, "Oh, I hope not."

Why, then, do people so often use the phrase, "It was God's will?" It is a simplistic answer to a complex question that they don't understand. They don't realize that you would be much more comforted if they said, "I don't understand it either."

When a child asks, "Why is the grass green?" it's easy to respond, "That's the way God made it." When the grass turns brown and looks dead, it's easy to give the same response. It quiets the child and provides an escape for the parent who may not have a scientific answer to the question.

God's role in what happened to you is your own faith decision. If you believe that somehow it was "God's will," that's fine. If that doesn't make sense to you, try to understand that those who say it mean well. They are nervous and anxious, and they want to be helpful. Their goal is to help you feel better, but they may not think before speaking. They may be sharing their own faith decision and are not trying to hurt you. What they want you to believe is that God still provides for you and cares for you.

It's Sinful to be Angry

Perhaps you grew up being told that it was bad to get angry. Just as Santa Claus or the Easter bunny might not come if you were "bad" or acted angry, God would reject you if you felt angry.

It is amazing that so many people believe that anger is bad when most religions address anger as a significant component in fighting or counteracting evil.

Why, then, are some people so eager to tell you piously that you should not be angry? Probably because they fear you might act on it. The thought of a suicide or homicide on your part, in response to the killing of your loved one, would be the ultimate trauma to those who love you. They will feel better if you can assure them that you will not make irrational decisions. Feeling rage, speaking in terms of revenge, or fantasizing about "doing in" the offender does not mean you are a vigilante or will act on your feelings.

It is extremely rare that persons deeply in grief make serious plans to kill the offender. They may think about it, but they very rarely commit a hostile or criminal act.

If your friends are so worried about your anger that they feel compelled to try to muzzle it, you can calm them by simply assuring them that you will not harm yourself or the offender. If you believe that the God of your faith can handle your anger, rage, thoughts about revenge, and confusion, tell them. You will feel better if you do, and so will they.

> Help! I can't stand this anymore!
> Get me out of here, God!
>
> The mud of my distress
> has sapped my strength,

disrupted my belief,
drowned my faith.

Where are you, God?
Why won't you rescue me
from this mire?

"Move over.

I don't promise to remove you
from the pain of living.
But I do ask you to give me room
to sit in the mud beside you.

Remember my promise to never leave you?
Trust me.
Move over."

– Dorothy Mercer

You Must Forgive.

Without a doubt, you will be called upon to rethink your concept of forgiveness. In order to survive the trauma and stay healthy, you will need to decide how to deal with your thoughts about the offender and maintain your integrity.

In killings in which the offender is also killed, the issue of forgiveness can be avoided to some degree. For those in which the offender remains alive, especially if the criminal justice system is involved in the case, the issue cannot be avoided.

Society tends to forgive easily. It is so eager to forgive that it doesn't require remorse on the part of the offender. Many homicides are plea-bargained in the criminal justice system, with the offender being advised by his or her attorney to plead guilty to a lesser offense in return for a more lenient sentence. At the same time, the offender is instructed not to make contact with you because it might imply an admission of guilt. Do society and the criminal justice system really believe that such a plea is genuine remorse? Apparently, they do. It is all that is required.

You and other family members may say, "If only he would look me in the eye and genuinely say 'I'm sorry,' it would mean all the world to me." A common reaction to this statement is that "only a vengeful family would put an offender through that." To you, hearing a statement of remorse and regret may be a very significant component of justice with integrity.

Some family members have been able to offer forgiveness when shown genuine remorse by an offender, even though they will never be able to forget. Many more, however, cannot forgive. Most are unwilling to offer "cheap grace" to offenders, a gesture of forgiveness that has no real meaning because the offender has shown no remorse and has made no commitment to change.

You will need to decide, based on your own life experiences and religious convictions, how you view forgiveness. It is a difficult and complex task. If others imply that you should be able to forgive, tell them it is an important matter, and that you will handle it in a manner compatible with your integrity.

Both the Hebrew scriptures and the New Testament of Christianity emphasize God's compassion for the abused and oppressed, not the oppressors. God opposes violence and supports it only in those cases where sin is rampant and sinners are unwilling to repent and change their ways, such as in Sodom and Gomorra. Jesus did not always forgive. In fact, He said "Whoever causes one of these little ones ('followers' in the Greek) who believe in me to sin, it would be better for him if a great millstone were hung around his neck and he were thrown into the sea." (Mark 9:42) Clearly, God stands with the sufferer.

Judith Herman, noted trauma counselor and researcher, has pointed out in her book, *Trauma and Recovery*, that both revenge and forgiveness can derive from attempts at empowerment. It is easy to understand vengeance as empowerment, even though the consequences of acting it out would likely strip the person of power. It is a little more complicated to think of forgiveness that way. The idea in its simplistic form, however, is that forgiving the offender should transcend the rage and diminish the impact of the trauma. Forgiveness is seen as a willed, positive act, while vengeance is understood as a willed, negative act. The myth is that one or the other will remove pain. Obviously, neither an act of hatred nor of love can fully transcend the trauma. Both are relational. Neither can be accomplished in isolation.

Love is unconditional. Forgiveness is not. Some say that forgiveness is divine. However, in nearly all religions, including Christianity and Judaism, forgiveness is conditional. Even a Japanese proverb points out that "Forgiving the unrepentant is like drawing pictures in the water." It is not an easy, simple one-time quick fix. It is a complex theological issue, and many believe that it should not be granted until the offender earns it through confession, repentance, and restitution.

It may be useful for you to realize that most references to forgiveness in the Bible are between God and a person, a restoration of a relationship that was broken. Jesus does not forgive the strangers gambling for his clothing at the foot of the cross. He asks God to do the forgiving, perhaps knowing that they have abandoned their relationship with God. Even in the stories of human forgiveness in the Bible, it is not granted simply at a whim. The father in the parable of the prodigal son does not seek out his son to offer him forgiveness while he is spending the family inheritance on wine, women, and song. It is only when the son realizes the foolishness of his ways and comes home, tells his father that he is sorry, and promises to change his ways, that the father embraces him and plans a welcoming party. In this story, forgiveness led to reconciliation of two people who originally loved each other and then fell out of relationship. Most family members of someone murdered never had a relationship with the offender in the first place, so what is there to be restored?

Psychological and theological issues are both at stake in what people call forgiveness. The word has different meanings for different people. Many use the word "forgiveness" for a process of psychologically "letting go." They choose to dismiss their concerns about the offender, determining that they will no longer allow that person to play a psychological role in their lives. The decision is unilateral.

An example of psychological letting go is Betty Jane Spencer, who has been quoted several times in this book. For years after her four sons were murdered, she was filled with rage for the offenders and for God. Through counseling, she was able to restore herself to and re-enter a relationship with God. She could set aside or let go of her rage toward the offenders, although she remained cautious because they continued to say that their only regret is that they did not kill her that night, too. Forgiveness, in the theological sense, did not seem appropriate to her because it implied a willingness to mutually enter a relationship with the offenders. She did not have a relationship with them before they murdered her family, and she had no desire to enter one. If they wished to restore their broken relationship with God, she was more than happy for them to do so. In the meantime, she no longer harbored negative feelings for them that might be detrimental to her.

David Augsburger, noted theologian and author of *Helping People Forgive*, further describes the mutual or bilateral nature of forgiveness as "experiencing healing and well-being by regaining the other as a brother or sister; celebrating restored or recreated relationships."

An example of bilateral forgiveness is Elizabeth Menkin, whose sister, Elaine, was killed by Suzana Cooper while Suzana was driving drunk. Elizabeth was filled with rage until the day she and her young niece went to look at the wrecked cars. Her niece noticed children's toys in the offender's minivan. They realized that the young woman who had killed their sister and aunt was a mother. Over the following weeks, Elizabeth's thoughts turned to the children whose mother was now in prison. She began to feel as if she had an unspoken relationship with the children, and, vicariously, with their young mother. At that point, she sought out a Victim-Offender Mediation program to prepare to meet with Suzana.

As she struggled to prepare for the meeting, Elizabeth Menkin pondered her Jewish faith and the "R's" of Yom Kippur: Recognition of having sinned, Remorse, Repentance, Restitution, and Reform. She could not offer Suzana Cooper forgiveness without evidence of these things on Suzana's part. She believed that God required these things of Suzana before she should consider forgiving her. Elizabeth became clear that forgiveness did not have to be given, but it could be earned. She thought she could offer it if it were earned.

Recognition, remorse, and repentance were apparent upon their first meeting, when Suzana could barely speak through her tears. Eventually, she accomplished the remaining two tasks as she entered a relationship with the Menkin family. During her 19 months in prison, Suzana was required to write to her own children every week, and to write to the victim's family quarterly, reporting on her progress. She was ordered to attend parenting classes and alcoholics anonymous meetings in prison, and to obtain her General Equivalency Degree (GED). When she was released, she was ordered to donate 10 percent of her earnings to charity, to go to church with her children, and to work to get other drunk drivers off the road. Nearly two years after Suzana's release, she was still doing well.

"Now, all I hope is that Suzana will eventually be able to view herself not as someone who did a terrible thing, but as one who, having made a terrible mistake, is now doing a courageous and honorable thing," says Elizabeth Menkin.

Forgiveness should be considered seriously. Theologian Dietrich Bonhoffer says that to do otherwise is to offer "cheap grace." Take your time and make it the right decision for yourself, your family, and the offender. The right decision is the one that stems from your personal integrity and faith. This decision may or may not be one that someone else feels is best for you.

If You Just "Turn It Over to God," You'll Be All Right.

Some may suggest that God is like a tranquilizer who will smooth the rough edges if you have enough faith. To make such a difficult task sound so simple may irritate you. Perhaps you have prayed, but your prayers did not seem to be answered. Or, you may have prayed and found a sense of calm and peace, but you are still confused. Veterans of faith in most religions find something of an "abiding presence" in the midst of their longing and suffering. They experience God not so much as a solution to their problem of grief, but as a Companion who stands with them in the midst of it. That kind of faith gives strength.

Because most of the people who love you feel inadequate to help you feel better, they wish that God would do it for them. They especially wish that their God would be present in you. Thus, words that may sound overly simplistic and trite actually may be expressions of their own genuine concern and love for you.

You may or may not believe that the soul of your loved one lives on in eternity. If you do, that, in itself, is consoling. It does not mean, however, that you do not have the right to miss and deeply long for the body and presence that you no longer can see, hear, or touch. Perhaps it will be helpful to you, as well as those who attempt to comfort you, to explain that there are many components of grieving, and that you are dealing with the religious components as honestly as you can. For example, you may find that after months or years, when you reach out to others you will find some of the answers.

> "Recently I asked Elie Wiesel how to overcome despair. We had been talking about things touching on despair, and on God. Hence my question. This man, who, more than most, has reason to despair, this man who lost his family in the death camp and himself barely survived, looked at me with those deep, dark eyes that have looked into the abyss and said, 'You want to know how to overcome despair? I will tell you. By helping others overcome despair.'
>
> He waited, then smiled a small smile. I realized the truth of what he'd said because I was feeling less despair in that moment precisely because he and I had talked together and shared together our struggles. He was saying that in that, I had helped him with his despair even as he helped me with mine. Eternal life and whatever hints at it is something we cannot have alone, only together."
> – *Theodore Loder, Pastor, First United Methodist Church of Germantown, PA*

After-Death Spiritual Experiences

Mystical-type experiences, where survivors sense the spiritual presence of their deceased loved one, are fairly common. They can be very spiritually and emotionally healing to those fortunate enough to have them.

Loved ones frequently report direct and spontaneous communication from their loved one. These communications range from a vague sense of the deceased person's presence to hearing voices, seeing visions (transparent figures to full bodies), feeling touches, and smelling aromas such as the loved one's perfume or after-shave. Verbal or unspoken communications frequently center around messages like, "I'm okay," "Don't grieve for me," "I love you," or a derivative of "Goodbye."

No one knows for sure if these reported occurrences are true messages from the deceased or merely a coincidence that was assigned meaning by the receiver. It is clear, though, that they offer reassurance and comfort to surviving loved ones.

> "Don't be surprised at very vivid dreams. I believe that Adrianne comes to me this way when she knows I need comfort. I think they come back to us, especially after a violent death, because so much is unresolved. They are just 'there.' There's no doubt about it. As time goes on, and as I become more healed, Adrianne's visits aren't as frequent or intense. I think she knows that if she didn't back out slowly and sweetly, it would be harder for me to go ahead and heal."
> – Linda Jones, whose daughter was murdered

If you have had an experience like this, accept it and celebrate it in whatever way you find meaningful. Share it with people you can trust. You will probably be surprised at the number of people who have had similar experiences. This phenomenon is discussed openly in many cultures of the world. Our society is so scientifically oriented that we easily lose touch with the mystical.

On the other hand, try not to despair if you have not had this kind of experience. No one knows why some do and others do not. It is probably unwise to seek out "psychics" to try to force this experience or to solve the crime. Some are legitimate, but many are not.

All of these issues of faith are an important part of your grief process. Processing them takes time and effort. By engaging them, you can feel satisfied that you are working through the spiritual component of your loss, which also affects the emotional component. It is hard work.

Suggestions

• Look for a person of faith who has had an experience similar to yours. Ask that person how their faith is helpful to them. You may or may not be able to share their experience.

• Avoid discussion with people who use God as a simple answer to complex questions. Try to accept the fact that their faith journey may be different from yours.

• Avoid conflict with people who are not comfortable with your anger and range of feelings. Assure them that you will not harm yourself or others.

• Try reading a few chapters from the Book of Psalms in the Bible, perhaps Psalms 23 and 139. Write in a journal or notebook what they mean to you.

• Think seriously about forgiveness and what you want it to mean to you and to the offender. Do not let anyone force you to say words you do not mean.

• If you continue to be troubled about religious feelings or beliefs, contact a hospital chaplain or a pastoral counselor within your own religion. Chaplains receive special training in accepting and dealing with traumatic grief. Or you can seek out a pastor, priest, rabbi or other faith leader who has previously been helpful to you or others.

What I Want to Remember From This Chapter

Chapter Eleven

PROFESSIONAL COUNSELING

It is not easy to decide if or when you need the help of a professional counselor to help you cope with your grief. Many people find that counseling is helpful, even if they feel they could get along without it. Counseling certainly will not hurt you if your counselor has some understanding of trauma following the sudden, violent death of a loved one and is committed to treating survivors with dignity and compassion.

As previously discussed, trauma grief shares many symptoms with clinical depression:

- Appetite changes

- Sleep disturbances

- Physical aches and pains

- Decreased sexual desire

- Loss of energy

- Inability to concentrate

- Need to withdraw

These natural consequences of grief following tragic loss can be misdiagnosed if the counselor is not fully aware of what you have experienced. However, just because they are common among those who have experienced a tragic death does not mean that you should not seek some symptom relief. Just as you take medicine to help you with a cold, flu, high blood pressure, or diabetes, it is fine to take medicine to help soften trauma grief symptoms as well. Many of these symptoms can be significantly eased with small doses of antidepressants. The newer ones do not make you feel groggy or zombie-like. In fact, it may take several days or weeks before you feel their effect. Even then, you may not feel anything dramatic. You just realize that it is easier for you to sleep, to get up feeling refreshed, to get through your work day, and to enjoy some of the things you enjoyed before.

Other common reactions among trauma survivors include:

- Unanticipated periods of crying (grief spasms) that can recur for years

- Occasional dreams and flashbacks

- Anger that is difficult to focus

- Difficulty deciding what to do with mementos, clothing and other possessions of the deceased

- Deep sadness, including irrational death wishes such as homicidal or suicidal fantasies

- Fear and anxiety, particularly about getting out in the community alone.

These symptoms should be considered natural and normal after a traumatic loss. It is rarely, if ever, appropriate to look at grief from the medical model, e.g., "You are sick and therefore require treatment to get well again." It is more appropriate to look at the severity of the trauma that caused the symptoms, and then decide if they are natural consequences of a very abnormal event.

No one knows for sure how long you should grieve, how many symptoms you should expect, or how intense a particular symptom will be for you. We do know that for most people, the grieving is painful and it lasts a long time.

It is even difficult to label your progress as you move through grief and begin to feel better. The word "recovery" sounds like you were sick and became well again. Very few people who have experienced the sudden, tragic death of someone they love ever feel completely "recovered." Most say they are changed by their loss. "Healing" is rarely complete, but it may be a more descriptive word of your goal because it at least implies that scars remain even after the open wound has closed.

It is crucial for you to realize that you will feel better over time. Time certainly does not "heal all wounds," but it does promote healing. The problem, however, is that we want to push the time it takes. We are a society of quick fixes, but there's no way that this will be fixed quickly. Anne Lamott says it well in her book, *Traveling Mercies*:

> "All those years I fell for the great palace lie that grief should be gotten over as quickly as possible and as privately. But, what I've discovered is that the lifelong fear of grief keeps us in a barren, isolated place, and that only grieving can heal grief. The passage of time will lessen the acuteness, but time alone, without the direct experience of grief, will not heal it."

Many survivors begin to rejuvenate on their own if they have family and friends who accept them, support them, and join them in their grieving. You will need to talk about the circumstances of the death and to share memories of your loved one over and over again. If your family or friends are unable or unwilling to be with you and hear you, you can find support from reading books like this one and by affiliating with organizations that provide grief support groups. Many survivors spend months or years in a support group as they regain emotional health. If a group is not available, or you find that a group does not help, you may decide to seek professional help. Some choose professional help along with support groups.

Most people know when they need professional help. They know because their physical symptoms are severe or because they are not improving. Some know they need help because their emotional pain is too difficult to endure. They are exhausted, but can't sleep because of disturbing thoughts, memories, or nightmares. Sleep deprivation leads to extreme irritability, anger outbursts, and depression. A professional counselor can help you assess your thoughts, feelings, and symptoms to determine if they are appropriate to your loss and grief. It is paradoxical that sometimes when you are feeling unsure, you are actually progressing well through your grief. If you are better today than you were a week ago or a month ago, you are probably making reasonable progress. If you are the same or worse, you will probably benefit from help.

The remainder of this chapter can serve as a checklist as you consider seeking the help of a professional counselor. Following are some of the symptoms that indicate you may need counseling and/or short-term prescription medication to help you to feel better. After a period of professional help, you may find that friends, family, and/or a support group are sufficient.

Getting "Stuck" in Grief

Grieving the loss of a loved one to a violent and unanticipated death continues, to some degree, for years. However, if you look over the last several months or years and see that your grief is just as intense now as it was immediately after the tragedy, you may be "stuck." The pain of having a loved one killed can take a while to surface. It can be more intense and last longer than the pain of most anticipated and non-violent deaths. If you cannot look back and see that you are getting better, or if you cannot imagine ever feeling better in the future, you may need professional help.

Absence of Grief

Not all people grieve openly. Some grieve privately and quietly, which makes other people think they are not grieving at all, and they worry that something is wrong with them. A small percentage of survivors actually do not grieve a great deal. They seem able to take trauma in stride. They may carry on, busy and efficient, and appear to be coping well. It is wise, however, if you are one of these people, to look carefully and sensitively at yourself. Do you feel anxious when you think of the one who was killed? Are you uncomfortable when friends offer sympathy? Do you forbid others to talk about your deceased loved one? Are you more tense and short-tempered than you were before? If you answered "yes" to some of these questions, you may benefit from help.

Nearly all people grieving the killing of a loved one go through a period when nothing about the death seems real. It is impossible to talk about it because the words just aren't there. The phrase "unspeakable terror" rings very true for these people. That is a natural reaction. In time, though, reality sinks in and words need to be spoken. Though difficult, it is healthy to lean into the pain and not fight it. When words do come, share them with someone who will accept them.

You may be afraid to think about your dead loved one because you think the pain will be intolerable. You may fear losing control. It is okay to avoid thinking about it for a while, but monitor your experience. If you are "carrying on as usual," but find that it takes a lot of energy to keep yourself from thinking about your dead loved one or to keep others from reminding you, you may need the help of a professional to support you as you begin to face reality. Failure to get help can manifest itself in emotional withdrawal from the people you love or in physical illness.

Pre-existing Problems

If you had problems before your loved one was killed, it is likely that those problems will increase. Health problems may get worse. If you have a history of mental or emotional problems, they may get worse. If your family or your marriage suffered problems, they may get worse. If you were a "loner" and didn't attract people to support you before, you will probably have difficulty attracting support now.

Sudden death in a dysfunctional family can be complex. Families in which members abuse alcohol or other drugs, families in which physical or sexual abuse are common, and even families in which one or both parents are workaholics are families in which denial reigns as a style of life. People in these families pretend that what's going on is not really happening. Many adults in dysfunctional families suffered deep emotional trauma as children. In order to cope with the chaos surrounding them, they learned to deny the pain. They learned to pretend. In fact, the worse things were at home, the more they pretended, and the better they looked and acted in public.

Unspoken rules in these families usually include, "Don't feel what you feel," "Don't talk about your pain," and "What happens in the family is the family's business and no one else's." If you grew up with these unspoken rules, it will be very hard to acknowledge what has happened and be willing to lean into the pain. For many, a courageous and painful journey back to childhood will be required before they can face the present grief. Under stress, most people resort to their lowest level of functioning. Members of a dysfunctional family are adept at appearing to stay in control in order to cover up the pain. That is exactly the opposite of what is required for grief work.

These facts need not discourage you. They simply mean that if you had problems in your family before the death, you are more likely than those who do not have these factors in their lives to need professional help. You must take responsibility to seek the help you and your family need.

Negative Self-Concept

Self-esteem can suffer when sudden violent death invades a family. Many survivors feel guilty and blame themselves for what happened. Most feel inadequate in trying to comfort others. Many wonder if they are strong enough to survive their grieving.

In time, however, rational thinking returns, and survivors are able to place responsibility appropriately. If you are unable to return to rational thinking or if you feel that you are bad, incompetent, and to blame, you probably need to talk these perceptions through with a professional counselor. Negative self-concepts and grief are a formidable combination, especially when they continue beyond normal expectations. You deserve help in coming to grips with them.

Excessive Guilt

Guilt, as noted previously, is normal for some time during the grief process. If your relationship with the one who was killed was good, you will likely be able to resolve your guilt in time. You will be able to remember the good times along with the bad times.

Longing and yearning for the person will still be a primary focus for a while.

On the other hand, if your relationship with the one who was killed was troubled, guilt may consume you. It can be so devastating that your conscience shoves it underground and forgets the bad times. Then, the hostility is no longer felt and the one killed is placed on a pedestal. This phenomenon is common when a teenager or the parent of a teenager is killed. Negative feelings are common as adolescents break away from the family. This also may happen when one partner in a troubled marriage is killed.

Sometimes, the guilt can be so severe that the survivor keeps the victim mentally alive in order to cope. In these cases, the deceased is referred to as if he or she is still alive. Most survivors have nightmares and flashbacks from which they emerge wondering if the victim really is dead. That is normal. However, if you believe, all the time, that your loved one is still alive, you need some professional help.

Sometimes survivors need to communicate with the deceased. They may devise magical rituals to communicate. Many survivors need time before they are able to sort through the clothing or dwelling of a loved one. However, people deeply in distress sometimes make a "shrine" of the things their loved one possessed or the room or house in which he lived. This survivor insists that the room be left exactly as it was before the loved one died, and becomes enraged if anyone attempts to move something. This survivor might attach magical significance to the room and touch certain things or look at particular objects as a means of seeking some kind of attachment to the deceased. A skilled counselor understands why a survivor finds it necessary to respond in this manner and will gently and patiently help the survivor to face issues that may free them to grieve more appropriately.

Dependency

Losing someone upon whom you are dependent is extremely traumatic.

A child whose parent has been killed cannot easily transfer dependence to a new caretaker.

Losing a child can devastate an elderly parent who depends on his adult child for care.

The spouse who relies on the mate for physical care, instruction, comfort, and support will be filled with stress, fear, and anxiety when forced to go it alone.

Some parents depend heavily on their child to fulfill their needs. A mother can feel that she is important only because her child needs her. Obviously, she will have a very difficult time coping if her child is killed.

Social support from family members and friends, and a transfer of emotional and physical needs to others who can be trusted to meet these needs are essential for a dependent survivor to get better. If these people are unavailable to you, find a professional counselor to help you find yourself again and learn a new way to live.

Suicide

Suicidal thoughts are not uncommon among the traumatically bereaved. As shock gives way to painful physical symptoms, deep anger, and great sadness, many survivors say they, too, long to die to escape the pain and/or to be reunited with their loved one. Most of them, however, will think rationally about the consequences of suicide and look for a more constructive way to cope.

One mother's despair overcame her to the degree that she took a gun to her daughter's grave, planning to commit suicide. As she swept the fallen snow from the headstone, she became keenly aware that she did not believe she would ever see her daughter again in eternity if she killed herself.

If your despair goes beyond a desire to simply not wake up in the morning, and you become pre-occupied with the idea of killing yourself, you must seek professional help. If you find yourself unable to think rationally, or if you have devised a plan for your own demise, you must tell someone. A counselor can help you find other ways to relieve the pain.

If you seriously contemplate suicide, you may find that your mind has become focused on the one who is likely to discover your body. You may be angry with that person and contemplate using the suicide to hurt him or her. A counselor can help you discover other ways of handling that problem.

If you have made up your mind to commit suicide, it will take strength and courage on your part to change your mind. For the sake of those who love you, you must stop yourself until you have at least visited a counselor to help you consider other alternatives. You may feel that there is no hope for feeling better. Even though you can't imagine it, you WILL feel better. The current pain is temporary. Suicide is permanent.

Finding a Good Counselor

It is sad but true that not all counselors or psychotherapists are skilled at trauma grief therapy. Therefore, you may need to shop around for the right counselor.

Word of mouth is the best referral source. Call the homicide or suicide support groups in your community and ask other survivors for the names of therapists they have found helpful. Many non-profit counseling and support groups such as Compassionate Friends, Parents of Murdered Children, Mothers Against Drunk Driving (MADD) know counselors with expertise in trauma grief. Your local Mental Health Association should be able to refer you to an appropriate counselor.

After obtaining counselor names, call several and ask the following questions:

1. Have you ever worked with clients whose loved one was killed? How many?

2. What kind of counseling do you do with people deeply in grief?

3. Under what circumstances do you arrange for prescription drugs?

4. About how many sessions do you have with a client who is having problems with grief?

5. What licenses or certifications do you have?

6. How much continuing education have you received during the last few years? Have you had any training in trauma grief therapy?

7. Do you provide individual counseling only or do you have victim support groups as well?

8. How much do you charge? Do you take insurance? Do you offer a sliding scale?

The most important rule in finding the right professional counselor is to trust your "gut" feelings. If, after two or three sessions, you do not feel supported, understood, and comfortable, you have the right to go elsewhere. You cannot get better in therapy unless you feel emotionally connected to the therapist in a way that makes you feel safe to share your thoughts and feelings honestly. Keep the following questions in mind throughout therapy:

• Do I sense that my therapist is competent to work with victims who are mourning sudden violent death?

• Do I feel that my therapist cares about me and recognizes my needs?

• Do I feel that I am making reasonable progress?

Therapy can be painful. A good counselor will support you as you work through the pain. You will find yourself looking forward to the sessions because you trust your counselor will treat you with dignity and compassion. If that does not happen, look elsewhere.

What I Want to Remember from This Chapter

Chapter Twelve

THE CRIMINAL JUSTICE SYSTEM

You may think that your sole task is coming to grips emotionally with all that has happened. Unfortunately, it is not.

Following a suicide, once the coroner or medical examiner rules it a suicide, the law enforcement agency that initially investigates the case usually closes it. After most murders and other killings, however, an offender is sought and sometimes apprehended. Whether apprehended or not, this situation adds another complex component to the grieving of surviving family members and friends.

Some offenders are never found. In these cases, the need for justice is thwarted and this gap can complicate grieving. It is difficult to focus anger when no one is clearly responsible. Feelings of helplessness and hopelessness can emerge. The anger can easily, if not always appropriately, be focused on law enforcement agencies that cannot locate the offender.

When the offender is also killed, survivors report mixed reactions. Some feel a sense of relief, although the relief does not diminish the grief for their loved one. Others deeply regret that the offender could not be punished by the criminal justice system.

If the offender was not killed and was apprehended, you likely will be thrust into the criminal justice system. It is against the law to kill someone intentionally, maliciously, or with criminal negligence. Therefore, the State has a responsibility to prosecute the offender for committing the crime, and to attempt to obtain a conviction.

As the surviving family, you probably are interested in obtaining justice and seeing the offender punished, even though no sentence seems just or adequate for what was done to your loved one.

The word "State" is significant. Your family is not a party to the criminal suit. The legal document reads "The State v. (Offender Name)." It does not read "(Victim Name) v. (Offender Name)." Unless you were present when your loved one was killed and, therefore, are an eyewitness to the offense, you will not automatically be involved in the case.

Most family members of the victim find the perceived detachment of criminal justice system personnel extremely frustrating. You may say, "It was not my State that was killed. It was my loved one!"

While that is true, it is the role of the State to punish the offender because he or she broke the law. You will learn more about bringing a personal lawsuit against the offender, a civil lawsuit, in the next chapter.

> "I can accept a great deal of ignorance and a great deal of lack of awareness--but to be told that I am not a real victim when I have lost something that is more precious to me than my own life, I will not tolerate. If you feel you are not dealing with real victims when you deal with homicide survivors, just call me."
> – *Dorothea Morefield, whose son was murdered*

Within the last couple of decades, the criminal justice system has involved the victim's family more in homicide and murder cases. A U.S. Supreme Court case has upheld the right of victims to testify about the impact of the crime on their lives. This generally happens during the sentencing portion of a trial, even in death penalty cases.

Crime victim families now have statutory rights in all 50 states and constitutional rights in about half the states to be present and heard during criminal proceedings, although a victim who is not a witness is still not a party to the criminal law suit. The victim's role has to do with the sentencing portion of the trial, not the fact-finding phase.

While these statutes and constitutional amendments vary from state to state, they generally include the following:

- the right to protection from intimidation from the offender

- the right to be notified of all hearings in the criminal justice process (although you must tell the victim advocate or prosecutor that you want to be informed)

- the right to information about Crime Victims Compensation and other victim services

- the right to give the prosecutor your opinion about proposed plea bargains

- the right to be present and heard during the trial

- the right to present a written (and in many states an oral) Victim Impact Statement before the offender is sentenced

- the right to an order of restitution to pay for your crime-related losses

- the right to be notified of probation and parole hearings

- the right to be notified of the release or escape of the offender from jail or prison.

Even though these laws are in place, not all prosecutors or representatives of the State grant these rights to the victim family. You may have to be assertive in order to claim them.

> "When my son was kidnapped, brutally beaten to death, and twice robbed, neither the law enforcement nor the justice system acknowledged the existence of survivors of homicide victims, let alone allowed them any rights. Although such sloppy treatment is not as widespread today as it was then, there still remains some die-hard resistance to the rights of survivors, even in those states where legislation provides for them. There is little or no recourse to that resistance and no effective reprimands for those who 'forget' to extend said rights."
> – *Janet Barton*

What Can You Do?

The Crime Report

The law enforcement agency that investigated the killing of your loved one prepares the crime report. If the crime happened within city limits, it is usually the City Police Department. The County Sheriff's Department generally investigates crimes committed outside the city limits. The State Highway Patrol investigates highway crashes outside the city limits.

Call the appropriate agency and ask how and when you can receive a copy of the crime report. Supplemental reports are filed as more investigation is conducted. Ask if, how, and when you may obtain copies of the supplemental reports. Do not expect to receive everything. Much of the information collected during the investigation must remain confidential until the trial is over.

The investigating officer should give you the identification number of the report, which is generally called the offense report. You may also request the badge number of the investigating officer. If you do not get the offense number, or if you lose it, you can obtain the report by providing the date and scene of the crime. Knowing the offender's name is helpful, but not essential. Look the report over closely for the following data:

- Do you see errors in the report? If so, report them immediately to the investigating officer whose name is at the bottom of the report. Even if the errors seem minor, they can be crucial to the court case.

- Are there indications on the report that the offender had been drinking or using other drugs when he or she killed your loved one? If so, look to see if a Blood Alcohol Content (BAC) level is indicated on the crime report. Breath, blood, or urine testing shortly after the crime was committed usually determines BAC. Breath test results are available sooner than blood or urine test results. If the tests were not performed, you have the right to know why they were not. These tests should be routinely given following automobile crashes in which alcohol or other drugs were used or suspected. Valid BAC testing can result in tougher penalties and sentences for drunk drivers.

Blood alcohol and drug levels are not as routinely tested in other homicide cases because of the usual lapse of time between committing the crime and apprehension of the offender. In some states, the consumption of alcohol or other drugs before or during the crime is considered a mitigating circumstance that may result in a more lenient sentence, if it is not a vehicular crime.

• Ask the investigator what charges are being recommended, why they were selected, and what elements of proof will be necessary to for a conviction.

• Ask when the investigating agency is likely to transfer the case to the prosecutor's office (sometimes referred to as the county attorney, district attorney, or state's attorney). Leave your name and phone number, and ask to be notified when the case is transferred. If you have not heard from someone within a few days after a case was expected to be transferred, call to inquire about the status of the case.

• Ask if the investigating agency has a victim assistance program. It is the victim assistance provider's role to keep you informed of the status of the case and to provide services you may need as a crime victim. Services include referrals to appropriate agencies, victim counseling, and assistance in applying to the State Victim Compensation Program for reimbursement of uninsured expenses resulting from the crime.

• If you are not satisfied with the information the investigating officer or victim assistance provider has offered, ask to speak with the investigating officer's supervisor.

Evidence

You may assume that the investigating officers have collected all the evidence they need. However, it is wise for you to document everything about the crime at the time it comes to your attention. You may think you will remember all the facts, but documentation will ensure a good recollection of all details.

• Additional witnesses may come forth who were not interviewed by the investigating officer. If so, refer them to the investigating officer or to the prosecutor, who will take their statement.

• Investigators probably took pictures at the crime scene and at the medical examiner's office. It is possible, however, that other pictures would be useful in both the criminal and civil case. A recent picture of your loved one before he or she was killed may be presented to the court prior to sentencing. It will personalize your loved one in the eyes of the court. If you take pictures after the crime was committed that you think may be helpful, have someone witness your actions. Sign and date the photos on the back, and ask the witness to do the same. Offer the photographs to the investigating officer or prosecutor.

• Ask for the return of clothing or personal effects that belonged to your loved one. These items may be in the investigator's office, hospital, or the medical examiner's office. Some of the items may need to be retained for the trial, but you should be given those that are not essential to the case. Ask about the condition of these things before opening the container to look at them. Their condition may differ from what you expect.

• Begin a record or log with receipts and bills of all your financial expenditures that were related to the killing of your loved one. These may include medical and funeral expenses, lost wages, fees for hiring a private investigator, and costs of professional counseling for family members. This information will be crucial if the offender is found guilty and the judge orders him to pay restitution to your family. It is also necessary in filing for State Crime Victim's compensation, insurance benefits, and civil suits.

The Prosecutor

After the investigating officer has transferred the case to the county attorney, district attorney, or state attorney, determine which prosecutor has been assigned to your case. If you know the name of the defendant, call the prosecutor's office and give that name so they can locate information about the case. Tell the victim assistance provider or secretary in the prosecutor's office that you want to be informed of what is happening during all stages of the criminal process. In most states, you will not be informed unless you specifically request this. Therefore, notify the prosecutor and/or the victim assistance provider in person or by phone of your desire to be informed. A written form may be provided for you to sign. Keep a log of all your calls.

After having requested notification by phone or in person, follow-up with a letter to both the prosecutor and the victim assistance provider, stating the name of the accused, your name, address, and phone number, your desire to be informed, the facts as you understand them about the case, and any feelings you have about bail for the accused, plea bargaining, or any other aspect of the case. Ask to be informed if the prosecutor changes the charge from its intended recommendation.

Charging

After reviewing the evidence in the case, the prosecutor may:

- File the criminal charges recommended by the investigating agency;

- File different, lesser, or additional charges; or

• Decide not to file charges because of insufficient evidence.

In most states, one of two procedures will determine whether probable cause or sufficient evidence exists to proceed to trial:

• A preliminary hearing may be held in which the prosecutor and possibly a few witnesses appear before the judge. If the judge determines that sufficient evidence exists, the accused will be scheduled for arraignment.

• A grand jury hearing is much the same as a preliminary hearing except the prosecutor presents evidence to a group of citizens rather than to a judge. Most grand juries are comprised of citizens who serve for several months at a time. Grand jury proceedings are closed to the public (including the victim's family). The accused is not present while others testify. The accused may or may not be called to testify. If the grand jury determines that sufficient evidence exists, they hand down a "true bill of indictment." If they do not think that sufficient evidence exists, the case is "no-billed." If indicted by the grand jury, the accused is scheduled for arraignment.

Arraignment

At the arraignment, the accused appears personally before a judge who informs him of the charges filed against him and of his constitutional rights, including the right to a court-appointed defense attorney. The accused is now called "the defendant" and will enter a plea of guilty or not guilty.

The Defense Attorney

The attorney for the defendant or one of his investigators may phone, write or appear on your doorstep. Before you communicate with any attorney or investigator, confirm his identity. Ask who he represents. A defense attorney is not a district attorney even though he may refer to himself as a DA. The defense attorney represents the rights of the accused and clearly is not there to represent your rights as a victim.

You do not have to speak to the defense attorney or investigator unless you are subpoenaed to do so. Ask him to get the requested information from the prosecutor's office. The prosecutor will accompany you if you are subpoenaed to give a deposition (statement) under oath.

Bail or Bond Hearing

Bail or bond is an amount of money given to a court by the defendant in exchange for his release and his promise to appear in court. Sometimes bond is set at the arraignment. Sometimes it is set at a separate hearing. The defendant can usually post bond through a bonding company for about 15% of the actual amount of bond set. If the offender is known by the victim, it can be very important for a representative of the victim family to be present when bond is set. This representative can inform the court of relevant facts concerning the defendant's likelihood to flee. Additionally, a family representative can address any potential danger to the family if the defendant is released from jail. This information could result in a higher bond or refusal of bond for a dangerous offender.

Discovery/Preliminary Hearings

After arraignment, the prosecutor and the defense attorney will gather evidence to support their cases. If the defendant has been arraigned on charges you do not understand, ask the prosecutor to explain to you the elements that must be proven to obtain a conviction. Hopefully, your prosecutor will discuss with you the strengths and weaknesses of the case. If you understand these, you may be able to provide additional information that will be helpful to the prosecution of the case. You may know of additional witnesses or have ideas about beneficial evidence. The prosecutor should know that you support him in trying to convict the defendant on the highest charges that can be proven. On the other hand, you must not turn yourself into an amateur investigator. If you get too involved, you may ruin or taint information or evidence that should only be sought by trained investigators.

Continuances

If you have properly requested to be informed of all proceedings, you should be notified of pre-trial hearings including requests for continuances (postponements of hearings). Pre-trial hearings are open to the public (including you), even though attorneys usually tell you it is not necessary for you to be there. Defense attorneys usually request numerous "continuances," or postponements, to "age the case." They know that the longer they can postpone the trial, the more likely the State will lose its witnesses, or witnesses' memories will fade. Ask the prosecutor to vigorously oppose unnecessary continuances at every opportunity.

In some states, the prosecutor may request a speedy trial on the basis of sensitivity to victims. (Defendants have a constitutional right to a speedy trial, but it is rarely in their interest to request it, especially if they have been released on bond.) In some states, the judge is required to state the reason for granting a continuance in the court record.

Continuances may be requested by the State or by the defense. They are often requested and granted for legitimate reasons, such as work conflicts or the unavailability of witnesses. Seeking or obtaining continuances does not necessarily mean that your case is being ignored.

> "Until the trial, you are constantly hitting a brick wall. The initial investigators treated us badly, as if we were totally ignorant. You know the cops and prosecutors know things that they aren't telling you, and when that happens, your imagination goes wild. Only when it's over can they be totally open with you. Now that I understand the reasons they had to withhold information, I would say it's a pretty good justice system. Our DAs were great in that they told us everything they could. When they can't tell you something, it's really important that they tell you why not."
> – *Linda Jones, whose daughter was shot and killed*

Plea Bargaining/Sentence Bargaining

These terms refer to negotiations that take place between the prosecutor and the defense attorney. Bargaining negotiations may result in a plea to a lesser charge or to a particular sentence in exchange for a reduced sentence. Bargains are usually distasteful to victim families who feel that to "cut a deal" is to betray the significance of the killing of their loved one. This is not always true.

In some circumstances, plea or sentencing bargaining is beneficial. If the preliminary investigation was inadequate, the offender may have been arraigned on a charge the State cannot now prove. It is better to allow the defendant to plead guilty to a lesser charge and to be punished, than to go to trial and risk losing everything.

Many states require that the victim's family be informed if plea or sentence bargains are considered. A few states allow the victim's family the right of input into bargaining decisions. Know your rights and assert yourself in claiming them. It is very important that you be present if a plea is presented to the judge. It will remind the Court that both the victim and the defendant should be considered in the decision rendered.

Victim Impact Statements

All states have enacted laws or procedures that allow family members of the victim to give a written or oral statement to the Court about the impact of the crime on their lives. These statements are presented after the defendant has been convicted and before he or she is sentenced.

Most states require the Adult Probation Department of their county to conduct a Pre-Sentence Investigation (PSI) on a defendant. The purpose of this investigation is to collect information before sentencing. A convicted offender may be sent to jail for a certain number of days, or to state prison for a few or many years. If the sentence is probated (served outside jail or prison), conditions of probation can vary widely. The defendant may be required to pay fines to the State. He may be required to pay restitution to the victim's family. He may be required to attend counseling, or a number of other options probation officers may recommend.

Until recently, pre-sentence investigations focused solely on the defendant. The victims' movement has succeeded in convincing many state legislatures that unless the victim's perspective also is presented, the court has not heard the whole story. The advent of Victims Impact Statements is a tangible result of this movement.

It is very important that Victim Impact Statements be prepared and presented to both the prosecutor and the probation department before a hearing to consider a plea bargain or sentence bargain. If the judge decides to accept a guilty plea, he may proceed immediately to sentencing. Therefore, it is essential that the judge have immediate access to the Victim Impact Statements.

Most states have a Victim Impact Statement form that can be requested from the prosecutor, probation department, or victim assistance provider. If not, simply write a description in letter form of the emotional and/or physical impact of the killing of your loved one on your family. Include any financial impact this egregious act has had on you. Include medical expenses, funeral expenses, lost wages, and any medical or counseling expenses that you incurred as a result of the crime. Documentation of these expenses can result in the defendant being ordered to reimburse you. If your state statute allows, you may also include your opinion about the defendant's sentence in your Victim Impact Statement.

> "Victim Impact Statements are a wonderful opportunity. This is the only time you can speak face to face with the offender who is, by then, a convicted criminal. Each of us thought carefully about what we wanted to say so we could stay calm and remind him of what he will remember every night when he goes to sleep."
> – *Linda Jones, whose daughter was shot and killed*

In preparing statements, be sure your information is accurate. Write from the heart about your pain, but try not to make bitter or disparaging remarks about the offender. Judgment of the defendant belongs to the judge or jury.

Mothers Against Drunk Driving (MADD) has a workbook to help you prepare your Victim Impact Statement. It is useful for any crime and can be obtained free from your local MADD chapter or by calling 1-800-GET MADD and speaking with a victim assistance provider.

Going to Trial

If the defendant persists in pleading not guilty, the case will be set for trial. The defendant has a constitutional right to choose whether the case will be decided by a judge (bench trial) or a jury. In most jurisdictions, the State must accept the form requested by the defendant. After a case is set for trial, be prepared for numerous postponements (continuances).

If the defendant chooses a jury trial, jury selection can take days or weeks before the trial actually begins. Most families choose to attend the trial, even though they know it will be an emotionally draining experience. Because trials can take several weeks, victim families may have difficulty getting off work to attend. Several states have now realized that victims should have the right to attend the trials concerning their loved ones without penalty, much the same as employees who are called to serve jury duty. Inquire about such statutes from your victim assistance provider or prosecutor. If no statute exists in your state, explain to your employer why it is important for you to be at the trial.

You may be surprised to learn that the defense may try to prevent you from attending the trial. One of the defense attorney's goals is to minimize sympathy for the victim during the trial. The defense wants sympathy to be focused on his client, the defendant.

A common tactic of the defense is to subpoena you as a potential witness, and then ask the judge to invoke the "gag rule," a rule stating that witnesses cannot listen to each other testify. Even though you may not be called to testify, you will, thereby, be kept out of the courtroom, never to be seen by the judge or jury. If you did not witness the crime and, therefore, would not testify until sentencing, ask the prosecutor to advocate that you be allowed in the courtroom.

> "Stephanie never let me down. I had to be there to be sure the court didn't let her down."
> – *Roberta Roper, whose daughter,*
> *a college senior, was murdered*

"I had to go. It was my responsibility to Andy and Pam. It would be evidence of their having been alive and loved."

– Louise Gilbert, whose son and
daughter-in-law were murdered

"I don't want to be at the trial, but I can't not be there. I don't want revenge, but I do want justice. And, I think that he should get the maximum if he's found guilty."

– Tinka Bloedow, whose 14-year-old
daughter was killed by a drunk driver

"We wanted to be there because no one was there to defend our daughter. The only picture the jury saw of Catina was the morgue picture. They had no idea what kind of girl she was. That's why it is so important that families be there, because the victim is not there to answer."

– Michael Salarno, whose 18-year-old
daughter, Catina, was murdered

Many states now allow victims (or victim's representatives and family members) to be present during the trial if they are not going to testify. If they are scheduled to testify, they are allowed to remain in the courtroom following their testimony. One state, Alabama, even allows the victim to sit with the prosecutor at counsel table, just as the defendant sits beside the defense attorney.

Some prosecutors worry that the victim's family may become emotionally upset during the trial and unduly prejudice the jury, providing grounds for a mistrial. If you want to be in the courtroom, assure the prosecutor that you will respect appropriate courtroom demeanor.

Be aware of these general courthouse guidelines because a violation of them could result in a mistrial:

• Do not discuss the case in the halls or restrooms. Your behavior out of the courtroom is as important as your behavior inside it.

• Never speak to judges or jurors, even if you encounter them in the hall, in the restroom, or at lunch. They must remain bias-free as they hear the evidence.

• Prepare yourself for the emotional impact of hearing the defendant say "not guilty." Even though you know you would not be in a trial unless he was pleading "not guilty," many victims report a jarring emotional reaction when they actually hear the words. In many cases, these are the first words the family hears the defendant speak.

• Expect to hear upsetting testimony. You may hear details about the death for the first time. You may see photos you have never been shown before. You may also hear the defense attorney attempt to show that your loved one was responsible for his or her own death. He has an ethical responsibility to do all he can to represent his client's legal interests. Therefore, much of what is important to you may seem like gamesmanship for players who try to outmaneuver each other in courtroom drama. It is up to the judge or jury to determine the truth.

• If you feel you may lose control of your emotions during the trial, leave the courtroom. Your demeanor in the courtroom must not be intended to influence the judge or jury.

• If you have questions or concerns during the trial, write them down and give them to the prosecutor or victim assistance provider during a break. Don't whisper during the trial.

• Victim assistance providers from the prosecutor's office or from support groups such as Mothers Against Drunk Driving, Parents of Murdered Children, or Compassionate Friends are usually available at your request to attend court proceedings with you and answer questions at appropriate breaks.

"The courtroom was a battlefield with combat played out between lawyers and a judge with a calm defendant dressed in his best."
— *Louise Gilbert, whose son and daughter-in-law were murdered*

"It was a nightmare, an absolute nightmare. When you learn of the death, you go into shock. At the trial, reality sets in. But, I still feel strongly that the family needs to be there."
— *Harriet Salarno, whose 18-year-old daughter was murdered*

"Finally, after a number of postponements, we sat in the small courtroom. I met the prosecutor and, moments later, came face to face with the man charged with killing my children. During the trial, I learned the meaning of horror, and their last hours were never again to leave my mind. Pam's fractured head and almost nude body were described in detail as well as the maggots and flies that covered her. I bolted the courtroom when the pathologist began to describe my son's bloated body."
— *Louise Gilbert, whose son and daughter-in-law were murdered*

Courtroom Procedure

Standard courtroom procedure during a criminal trial is as follows:

• Both attorneys give opening statements.

• The State calls witnesses to the stand in an attempt to prove that the defendant is guilty as charged. The prosecutor's questioning of each State witness is called "direct examination." The witness is then "cross-examined" by the defense attorney. The procedural rules for cross-examination are more liberal than rules for direct-examination. For example, in cross-examination, leading questions may be asked such as "Isn't it true that....?" After cross-examination, the witness is given "re-direct examination" by the prosecutor and "re-cross examination" by the defense. The witness is then dismissed, unless either attorney plans to call the witness back to testify later. Once dismissed, witnesses may usually remain in the courtroom. However, it is prudent to sit near the back of the courtroom out of the direct view of the judge or jury.

• After the State has presented all its witnesses, the defense will present its witnesses, going through the same process of direct and cross-examinations.

• After all the evidence has been presented, each side may introduce witnesses to rebut previously given testimony. Rebuttal witnesses can be witnesses who have previously testified but have not been dismissed, or they can be new witnesses.

• Each side presents closing arguments. The State has the burden of proof in the case and therefore has the right to argue both before and after the defense. Typically, the prosecutor will summarize the evidence before the defense argues. Then the prosecutor will rebut the defense's arguments.

• The judge gives the jury instructions for their deliberations, or if it is a bench trial, retires to deliberate himself.

The Verdict

Hearing the announcement of the verdict is the climax of the trial and is usually a very emotionally-laden time for the victim's family. You must be aware that a legal verdict and the truth are, unfortunately, not always the same. While a defendant may not, in truth, be innocent, he may be proven "not guilty." Judges and juries are the best way our society knows to determine legal justice. Judges and juries are also susceptible to human error. All of this must be kept in perspective.

The standard of proof in criminal cases is "beyond a reasonable doubt," the highest burden of proof required in any trial proceeding. This term is legally undefined. However, if any doubt based on reason exists as to any element of the offense as charged, the verdict of the judge or jury must be "not guilty" on that offense. Evidence must establish the facts so clearly, positively, and explicitly that there can be no reasonable doubt that the case was proven.

Sentencing Trial or Hearing

If the defendant is convicted, the case will proceed to sentencing. Sentencing may occur immediately following the conviction or be scheduled for a later date. Even though you did not witness the crime, you may be allowed to testify during the sentencing hearing.

Written Victim Impact Statements are submitted to the prosecutor and probation departments before sentencing. A representative of these departments passes the statements on to the judge for consideration in sentencing. If oral impact statements are allowed in your jurisdiction, you may be called to the witness stand to testify about the impact of the crime on your life.

> "The prosecutor put me on the stand. He wanted the jury to hear first-hand about the devastating effect the killing of Stephanie had on our family. Defense objected. After a brief conference, the judge agreed with the defense that legally, Stephanie's character and our grief were irrelevant.
>
> I had been silenced. Yet, the defendant's former teacher and his prison minister would both speak on the defendant's behalf. The court deemed their statements relevant. I burned with anger."
>
> – *Roberta Roper, whose daughter was murdered and who later introduced legislation, now law in Maryland, that Victim Impact Statements must be heard. The right has now been upheld by the U.S. Supreme Court as well.*

Evidence and procedures differ during sentencing, which is sometimes called the dispositional phase of the trial. Defense witnesses will be called to provide subjective testimony about the defendant and why they feel he should receive a particular sentence.

Since the goal of your Victim Impact Statement is to convey the effect your loved one's killing has had on you, it is not expected that you testify during this phase free of emotion. Be aware, however, that judges and juries can tell the difference between genuine and contrived emotion.

You need not fear testifying if you discuss your testimony honestly with the prosecutor and think through how you want to present it. Following are some suggestions that should help you testify with relative ease and maximum credibility:

• Dress conservatively. Wear a business suit if you are a man, or a dress or business suit if you are a woman. Your clothing, jewelry, and hairstyle should not be flashy or in any way detract from what you are saying.

• Take notes or a written statement with you to the witness stand if you think you may need them. However, be aware that the judge, attorneys, and jury may be allowed to examine them. Don't have anything on your notes that could embarrass you.

• If the defense attorney asks if you have discussed your testimony with your attorney, it is appropriate to respond, "yes." Your attorney may have helped you organize your statement, but you prepared your statement yourself and are testifying to the true impact of the killing on you and your family.

• If you don't understand a question by one of the attorneys, simply say so and ask that it be repeated. If you do not know the answer to a question, say so. If you feel an attorney is trying to manipulate you into an answer that is not true, turn to the judge and tell him that you will need to explain your answer.

• Be descriptive as you speak of the impact of the killing. Describe particular events that were/are painful for you. Your goal is to enable the judge or jury to come as close as possible to understanding how you felt when it happened and how you feel now.

• Do not use jargon or judgmental words if you say anything about the offender. Words such as "drunk," "alcoholic" and "crazy" are judgmental words you should not use. Talk about your pain and avoid bitter or disparaging remarks about the defendant.

• Avoid unnecessary phrases or cliches such as "I honestly believe that...." or " I can truthfully say that....". They are not as powerful than short, simple statements.

• Maintain eye contact with the attorney who asks you the question. Don't look to your own attorney for help when being questioned by the defense attorney. Look at the judge or jury only if the attorney asks you to explain something to them.

• If you request that the defendant pay restitution to your family, be prepared to present actual bills and statements of the amounts paid or owed.

• Always be honest. Take your time. Pauses before your answers indicate that you are taking the question seriously and thinking before you speak. If you approach the task of testifying with integrity, your testimony will be respected.

Appeals

Following a conviction and sentencing, the defendant has a right to appeal the findings of the case to a higher court, and to ask for review of errors in procedure or application of the law at the trial court level. Be prepared for this phase, especially if the sentence is maximal. After an appeal is filed, many convicted felons are released on appeal bonds until the appeal is heard, which may be several years later. Under the concept of "innocent until proven guilty," a trial court decision is not considered final until appeals are heard. While this hardly appears fair from the victim's perspective, it is a procedural safeguard that has proven useful, especially when a convicted defendant is innocent.

Sentences handed down are seldom sentences served. "Good time," credit given for days of imprisonment because of good behavior, is common. The convicted criminal may actually receive two or three days' credit for each day served, and in fact, serve only a fraction of the actual sentence imposed. The prison system benefits several ways from offering good time. It motivates prisoners to act appropriately and follow the rules while in prison, and it gets them out of the system sooner, helping to alleviate prison overcrowding.

> "Judge Haile gave Jones a life sentence for murder, a life sentence for rape, and twenty years for kidnapping. But, surprising even the defense, he announced that the sentences could be served concurrently. This meant that Jones would be eligible for parole in less than twelve years with credit for time already served and credit for good behavior."
>
> *– Roberta Roper, whose daughter was murdered*

"The boy who killed our daughter was a juvenile (17). He was found guilty of criminal negligence involving a death, drunken driving, and hit and run. He was sentenced to 90 days in a chemical dependency treatment and behavior modification program, his license suspended for six months, and he was placed on probation until his nineteenth birthday.

I later learned that he was again charged with drunk driving when he was 21. The previous conviction had not been reported to the Public Safety Department, and the new charge was being treated as a first time misdemeanor. When I finally got them to look into it, I learned that within six months of his license being reinstated, he had had two speeding violations and another for driving with an open bottle. We got his license suspended again, but when the suspension was over, he was cited for an illegal turn and use of a motor vehicle in commission of a felony. Following yet another license revocation, he was cited with refusing a breathalyzer test following a drunk driving arrest. I'm enraged, absolutely enraged. I thought the system worked, but I'm not so sure now."

– Tinka Bloedow, whose daughter
was killed by a drunk driver

As soon as the convicted offender is placed in jail or prison, call the victim assistance provider at the sheriff's office (or entity responsible for the county jail) or the victim assistance provider at the prison to obtain his identification number. Include this personal identification number (PIN) and his full name in all correspondence with parole boards. Always include your own name and address so you can receive a response.

Send a copy of your original Victim Impact Statement to the Parole Board. Write the parole commissioners responsible for the particular facility to which the prisoner is assigned as well as the State Parole Board. Inform the Parole Board in writing from time to time about the ongoing impact of the death of your loved one. Especially send new letters when it is time for parole review. Petitions submitted requesting continuing incarceration can be very important at review time because they represent the views of the community. Call prior to the review and ask if you may provide an oral statement. In any event, leave your phone number and ask to be informed when the review decision is made.

Many jails and prisons have now incorporated an electronic notification system that automatically places a call to you when there is any proposed change in the offender's status. This simplifies notification because it is automatic. However, unless you are in the system, you will not be called. If this service (many are called VINE systems) is available for you, the victim assistance providers who work with you will know how you can register.

Cases Against Juveniles

In most states, juvenile hearings are not open to the public, including the victim's family. Juvenile case files are closed. With increased frequency, however, victims of juvenile offenders are granted many of the same rights as victims of adult offenders. If the offender in your case is a juvenile, inquire right away about your rights as a victim. You can do this by contacting your law enforcement victim assistance provider or a juvenile probation victim assistance provider.

Other Resources

Writing Letters

Letter writing should follow every interaction you have with the criminal justice system. Since a conversation may be forgotten, undocumented, or misconstrued, it is always wise to follow up with a letter. It can prevent a prosecutor, probation, or parole officer from saying "I don't remember you saying..." or "I was never informed."

The League of Women Voters suggests that, as you think about your letter, you consider the sentence, "_____ wants you to _____ because _____." Consolidating your concerns into this format will help you keep your letters clear and persuasive. Use short sentences and short paragraphs. Use action verbs such as "urge" rather than "wish." Be polite and respectful.

Never write a letter to the judge until the offender has been found guilty. Victim Impact Statements go to the prosecutor and probation department, who will present them to the judge at the appropriate time for the sentencing hearing or trial.

The Media

If the killing of your loved one was sensational, or if the criminal case is unique, the media may be eager to present it in written or broadcast form. It is your right to choose whether to speak with the media. If you decide to do so, it is best to contact your prosecutor first. You don't want to jeopardize your case in any way by what you might say in public. Sometimes, excessive publicity can result in a change of location (change of venue) for the trial. Media communication during a trial can cause a mistrial, especially if the jury is not sequestered (kept together day and night to avoid being influenced by others or by what they read or watch on television).

If you do obtain the prosecutor's permission to speak with the media, be certain that you have your facts straight and that you refer to the defendant as the "accused" or "alleged criminal" until conviction. He or she is not a criminal or a felon until the court has made that determination through a guilty verdict. If you speak to a newspaper reporter, you may ask that the reporter call you and read the article to you before it goes to the copy editor, but most reporters will not do so. The reason is that they lose control of their story once it goes to the copy editor, so it is not likely to reach final print in the form they submit it. If you feel that gross errors or misstatements have been made, you may call the reporter or the reporter's supervisor, but most often, it is not the reporter's fault.

Remember: It is always your right to turn down an interview with the media or refer reporters who have questions to the prosecutor who is handling your case. Avoiding media questions until after the trial is usually the best policy.

An effective strategy for handling the media is to seek out a victim assistance provider (or a family member or friend) who has media expertise to serve as your spokesperson or media representative. Once acquired, simply put a message on your answering machine indicating that all media calls are to be directed to that person. Use Caller ID and do not pick up the telephone unless it is someone you know and want to talk with. Your media representative will screen the calls and will call you only when necessary to see if you choose to respond to any inquires. If so, he or she will help you draft a response. Your prosecutor's victim assistance provider can help you locate a spokesperson.

Ethical Review Procedures

While the caliber of attorneys in a typical prosecutor's office is high, review procedures are available in most jurisdictions to investigate the conduct of individuals if you feel they have been unethical in the treatment of your case.

Most states have a Prosecutor's Council or similarly named investigative group to look into complaints about prosecutors. Local and state bar associations have procedures for investigating complaints and taking appropriate actions. Attorneys may be disbarred or reprimanded by the State Supreme Court in many states.

Most states have Judicial Conduct Commissions to investigate judicial misconduct. The State Attorney General's office investigates professional misconduct on the part of employees of the State. If you use these avenues, be sure that you have your facts straight before filing a complaint.

Conclusion

Becoming an active player in the criminal justice system can add stress to your grief. You may decide that you aren't up to it and choose to let justice take its own course without your involvement. On the other hand, working with your case may be an essential component in your emotional pilgrimage to get better.

Some say that, regardless of the outcome, participating in the criminal justice system gave them a sense of completeness. It will not cause you to grieve any less or erase the imprint of your loved one's killing on your life, but it may give you some sense of accomplishment and the knowledge that you did everything you could for your loved one.

The final disposition of the case can provide a historical perspective that will enable you to focus less on the offender and more on yourself and your journey toward feeling better about life.

What I Want to Remember From This Chapter

Chapter Thirteen

FINANCIAL ISSUES

"Those first few days after my daughter's murder, I remember feeling that people only wanted money. Everywhere we went, we were asked for cash and nobody seemed to care why we were there."
  – Wanda Lawendel Bincer, whose
    daughter and son-in-law were murdered

The financial outlay required when a loved one has been killed can make you feel victimized yet again. It is unfair that you should have to pay both emotionally and financially for someone else's malicious or negligent act. This chapter provides information about sources of financial assistance after a loved one is killed. However, it is not intended to substitute for experienced financial or legal advisement.

Final medical bills, funeral expenses, travel and telephone expenses, and lost wages can seem unending and overwhelming. If the person killed was a primary source of family income, immediate financial assistance may be critical.

Fortunately, others can help you with your financial matters. First of all, do not hesitate to call on other responsible family members, trusted friends, or a professional financial advisor. These people are usually standing ready to help you, even though you may be uncomfortable asking. If a trusted friend or relative is willing, ask him or her to handle all the bills for awhile. These bills can seem like another wave of victimization. Decide when you are ready to resume responsibility for your financial affairs.

The Funeral

For many families, simply paying for an unexpected funeral seems impossible. Most funerals cost more than $5000. State Crime Victim Compensation funds are available in most states to pay for or assist in paying for the funeral of someone who died as a result of crime that was not their fault. If the funeral home is not aware of this program, ask that they contact the victim assistance program of the local law enforcement agency or prosecutor's office for information. Once they know that they will eventually be paid, most are willing to conduct the funeral and burial. In addition to paying for the funeral, Emergency Crime Victim Compensation funds are available in most states to assist victims with immediate financial needs that may arise before regular benefits are awarded. If needed, discuss this with the victim assistance provider as well. If you will be applying for Crime Victim Compensation funds, it is crucial that you set up a file and keep receipts of all expenditures that are related to the crime. You will only be reimbursed for expenses for which you have receipts.

Documents

An important next step is to locate the will, insurance policies, trusts, tax returns, checkbooks, and information about stocks, bonds, and real estate owned by the victim. Check desks, file cabinets, and safe deposit boxes, if you have access.

In order to complete applications for various claims for financial recovery after a death, request at least twelve original copies of the certified death certificate from the funeral home. If your spouse was killed, copies of the marriage license, social security cards of all family members, birth certificates of minor children, and military discharge papers will be required as well.

Cash

The easiest way to access cash is from checking and savings accounts, money market funds, certificates of deposit, mutual funds, stocks, and bonds. Be aware, however, that penalties may be imposed if you use the money prematurely. If the deceased had a stockbroker or financial planner who managed all these funds, you will be fortunate because he or she can help you sort out your wisest options.

All banks in which your loved one had accounts must be notified immediately after the death, but no one will have access to these accounts until an administrator is appointed. If spouses held a joint account, the surviving spouse may have access up to a certain amount. If a joint account holds a large sum of money, a waiver may be signed to gain access to the money. The names on the joint account will now need to be changed to the widow or widower's name.

A safe deposit box rented jointly or in the name of the deceased is sealed at the time of death. Requests to access to insurance policies or other legal documents in the safe deposit box must be signed and witnessed.

Social Security/Veterans Benefits

These benefits are available to survivors to replace, in part, family earnings lost when a wage earner dies. You should apply for survivors benefits promptly because, in some cases, benefits will be paid from the time you apply and not from the time your loved one died. The website, *www.socialsecurity.gov,* is a valuable resource for information about all Social Security programs. You also can call toll-free at *1-800-772-1213,* where staff can answer specific questions and provide information by automated phone service 24 hours a day. If you are deaf or hard of hearing, you may call the TTY number, *1-800-325-0778.*

You can apply by telephone or at any Social Security office. The nearest office will be listed in your phone book. If your loved one was a veteran, the nearest Veterans Administration office will also be listed in the phone book, or you can call *1-800-827-1000.* These agencies will need either the following original documents or copies certified by the agency that issued them:

- Proof of death—either from a funeral home or death certificate;

- Your Social Security number, as well as the deceased's;

- Your birth certificate;

- Your marriage certificate, if you are a widow or widower;

- Your divorce papers, if you are applying as a divorced widow or widower;

- Dependent children's Social Security numbers, if available;

- Deceased worker's W-2 forms or federal self-employment tax return for the most recent year; and

- The name of your bank and your account number so your benefits can be deposited directly into your account.

If you are already getting benefits as a wife or husband based on your spouse's work, when you report the death, the agency will change your payments to survivor benefits. If the person who was killed was already drawing benefits and a check written to him or her arrives after the death, you must return it. If it is made out to the deceased and to you jointly, you may take it to the nearest office, and it will be stamped so you can cash it.

Life and Medical Insurance Policies

The money from a life insurance death benefit, payable to a specific beneficiary, should be immediately and automatically available to the beneficiary, even if premiums were not paid after the death. However, delays are common, especially if suicide is still being considered as a possible cause of death.

Read each policy carefully before filing a claim. Some life insurance policies include double or triple indemnity benefits if the insured dies catastrophically. Many policies include an "incontestability clause" that states that the insurance company cannot dispute the validity of a policy after it has been in force for a specified period.

Check everywhere that records of the deceased may have been stored to be sure all policies are located. Contact the family attorney, financial planner, banker, accountant, and employer. Millions of insurance benefits go uncollected every year because no one knew about the policies. In addition to policies related to employment, some unions and professional organizations offer group life and/or health insurance to their members. Carefully examine health and hospital insurance policies to be sure you know how to file a claim for payment of final medical expenses.

If the person killed or injured was in a vehicular crash, the driver's automobile insurance should pay most of the final medical bills. The victim's own health care plan should pick up the remainder. After all the policies of the deceased have been located and examined, notify each insurance company of the death and request the appropriate claim forms. Then check any other existing policies in which the deceased was named as a beneficiary and change the beneficiary name. The names on automobile insurance policies will also need to be changed.

Employer Benefits

Sometimes, surviving family members do not know about employer policies because the policies are not stored at home. Contact the benefits specialists in the personnel department of the victim's employer about all benefits, sick leave pay, accrued vacation time pay, unpaid bonuses, and the final paycheck. Ask if you need to sign forms and when you should expect to receive the money. If the deceased was covered by an employer-funded pension plan, you may be entitled to monthly payments or a lump sum payment that can be rolled over into an IRA. Death benefits from 401(K) or 401 (b) plans, tax-sheltered annuities or Keogh plans (self-employed) typically are paid out in a lump sum or can be rolled over into a tax-free IRA by the surviving spouse. Other benefits will be taxed.

If dependents are covered on a health insurance policy of the deceased, determine how long the coverage will continue. If coverage does not continue after a certain date, ask about options for a continuation policy for dependents under the Consolidated Omnibus Budget Reconciliation Act (COBRA). COBRA generally applies only to companies with 20 or more employees. You must apply for these extended benefits within 60 days, so timing is crucial. Group health coverage for COBRA participants is usually more expensive than health coverage for active employees, since the employer generally pays a part of the premium for active employees while COBRA participants pay the entire premium themselves. It is ordinarily less expensive, though, than individual health coverage. You may learn more about COBRA at *www.dol.gov/ebsa/faqs/faq_consumer_cobra* .

Also check with the deceased's former employers to see if benefits such as pensions or life insurance policies purchased while there are available to the survivors.

If the surviving spouse is employed, his or her policies also should be checked. The deceased may have been covered by those policies. After all claims relative to the death are filed, a new beneficiary will have to be named. Check all health policies to see if mental health counseling is paid for, in the event it is needed.

Get clarification from your own employer about how your time away from the office will be documented and paid. You may need time off from work to visit attorneys, attend court hearings, and attend to the multitude of other matters that can be dealt with only during the daytime. Ask if a subpoena is required if you plan to attend court, or if you will be penalized for time away from your job.

In most states, the family of an employee killed on the job is entitled to Worker's Compensation benefits. Inquire about this through your employer if the death was job-related.

Creditor Intervention

The unanticipated death of a family member nearly always requires that ongoing bills be set aside while immediate expenses are paid. While it can be difficult, it is important to contact the deceased's creditors by phone and tell them what has happened. Check all loan contracts, mortgages, and credit card contracts to see if there is a clause that addresses payment of the balance in case of death. The common language of these funds is credit or mortgage life insurance. If these benefits are identified, notify the creditor immediately and request claim forms.

Next, list all creditors, their addresses, and the amount owed. Then consider the amount remaining after paying immediate expenses. Determine how much ongoing income and lump sum payments are expected. Be cautious about accepting inadequate insurance settlements out of fear of facing creditors.

From these figures, determine how much, if anything, can be paid on bills in the near future. Write each creditor. Explain what has happened and advise the company of the amount you can pay each month and when payment can be expected. State that you are proposing a new payment schedule that will fit both your need and the creditor's, and that, if you do not hear otherwise, you will assume that the creditor agrees with the plan you have submitted. Make copies of these letters for your files.

In cases where accounts are joint, inform creditors that the name on the account should now be changed to your name. A surviving spouse should not assume responsibility for credit cards in the name of the deceased spouse only. Credit card companies are persistent in requesting widows and widowers to sign their spouse's debts over to themselves.

In some cases, emergency funds are available for bills. Public utilities such as the electricity, gas, or water company may extend credit if an application is completed.

In the event that a landlord is uncooperative, phone your City Offices and ask for the department that handles landlord/tenant relations. Request a copy of regulations or ask how to access them on the Internet. Most Legal Aid services also have summaries of these regulations.

It is to the creditor's advantage to work out payment schedules so he is eventually reimbursed. It is also against the law in most states for a creditor to harass or intimidate a debtor. IF the creditor refuses to accept the payment plan, write another letter and send a copy to your attorney. If that fails, ask a Legal Aid service or attorney, hired on an hourly rate basis, to intervene on your behalf.

Automobile Insurance Benefits

Insurance practices differ from state to state. If residing in a no-fault state, costs are covered by the policy of each individual involved in the crash. This holds true even if the driver was driving someone else's vehicle. Check your state Insurance Code on the Internet or call your State Insurance Commission at the State Capitol for defined coverage time and dollar limits. In addition to death benefits, property benefits, medical benefits, and funeral costs, inquire about the use of a rental car, wage loss, replacement costs for services such as child care and housekeeping, and mental health counseling benefits.

If family members were injured but survive, inquire about their lost wages, rehabilitation expenses, and replacement services as well as medical benefits.

In a no-fault state, if the driver of an automobile was liable for the crash and has liability insurance, you probably will receive benefits from the liability insurance company. Eligibility conditions vary based on the insurance laws in the each state.

If the driver liable for the crash had no liability insurance at the time of the crash, you may be eligible to receive benefits from the uninsured/underinsured motorist provisions of the deceased's policy. Again, the insurance laws of each state and the specifics of the policy will define that eligibility.

Insurance adjustors may approach you soon after the crash. Decisions made at that time may have far-reaching financial ramifications. Be cautious:

> • If you have chosen to retain a civil attorney (It should be one who specializes in wrongful death cases), refer all insurance representatives to the attorney. This

includes the adjustor of your own insurance company.

• If you choose to handle the claim on your own, be sure you know the company of the adjustor with whom you are dealing. If an adjustor comes to your home, ask to see a business card. If the adjustor's language is confusing, say so. Even though you may choose to discuss the case, it is wise not to give signed or recorded statements until you are absolutely certain about what you are signing.

• Be fully competent and aware when you discuss the case with an insurance adjustor. Grieving can make you feel numb and confused. It can cause your memory to fail. If you are not able to discuss the case rationally with the adjustor, ask him or her to return at another time. It is a good idea to have a trusted person with you when you discuss these matters.

• Keep copies of crash reports, repair estimates, medical and funeral bills, and copies of letters relating to the insurance settlement in a separate insurance file.

• Get several estimates on damage to the vehicle before settling on property damage. These may be obtained from body shops or automobile dealers. You can negotiate the insurer's offer if you have several estimates.

• Obtain copies of all medical bills before settling on the medical or bodily injury damages. If others in your family survived the crash, it is very important to know the full extent of injury and prognosis for treatment before making a final settlement. This may take months. Keep a daily record of adverse effects of the crash, including psychological impact. Be sure that when doctors write medical assessments, they understand the injured victim's former job description, employment history, and educational level.

• As you discuss the insurance settlement, the company may alter their offer. Request a copy of each settlement offer in writing to avoid confusion or conflicting information. It does not need to be a formal word-processed letter, but may be handwritten, signed, and dated by the person making the offer.

• The adjustor may or may not be able to advise you of your claim rights based on statutory insurance law, since insurance adjustors do not have legal degrees. You may ask to have a written copy of claim rights in your state. Be sure you know the statute of limitations for personal injury and property damage actions in your state. You may want to consult an attorney on an hourly fee basis for this information.

If you feel that a claims adjustor is not treating you properly, contact his or her supervisor. If that is not satisfactory, write a personal and confidential letter to the president of the insurance company, describing your experience. Your State Insurance Commission or State Board of Insurance may also be contacted. All legitimate insurance companies are regulated by the State Insurance Commissions of the states in which they sell insurance. Contact the switchboard at your State Capitol for the phone number or use the browser on your computer to find their website. All telephone or personal communication about your complaint should be followed by a written letter that summarizes the communication.

In most states, insurance companies are required by statute to act in "good faith." This mean that if claims are unreasonably denied, if valid claims are not promptly paid, or if families are coerced into settling for less than is due them, this behavior gives rise to a course of action against the insurance company. Punitive damages may also be recoverable upon proof of actual malice, fraud, or oppression, usually referred to as "outrageous conduct." Sometimes, a victim is forced to sue his or her own insurance company.

Homeowner's or Renter's Insurance

Your homeowner's or renter's insurance probably will cover the content from the home, or, if a vehicular crash, from the vehicle including luggage, purses, or damaged clothing. These items, however, will likely be subject to a deductible. Contact your insurer to learn how to apply for reimbursement. Usually an itemized list of lost or damaged items, their age, and approximate purchase price is required.

Umbrella Liability Insurance

If the offender has an umbrella policy, it will pay for damages that extend beyond the liability limits of homeowner, renter, or automobile policies. These policies usually carry a maximum $1 million in coverage, but you may have to file a lawsuit to get the money.

Civil Wrongful Death Suits

If the person responsible for the death of your loved one has substantial income or assets which are recoverable, or if the liability insurance company has failed to offer a fair settlement for a claim, consider filing a wrongful death civil suit.

Civil actions are separate from the criminal case. While the State provides a prosecutor to try the criminal case, you will have to hire an attorney for a civil proceeding. Do not expect either attorney to advise on the other suit, although they should be interested in each other's cases to enhance their own. Civil actions depend largely on the way the death occurred and financial expenses incurred. Recovery of medical, funeral, and property expenses are usually the first to come to mind. Financial recovery may be possible for other damages such as past and future wage loss including retirement benefits, and past and future pain and suffering. In some states, if one spouse is killed, the other spouse can sue for loss of consortium (change in relationship). Some states also allow for punitive damages, additional money to punish the offender.

If a public entity such as the City, County, or State Government was responsible in any way for the death through commission or negligence, financial recovery may be possible from them as well. Traditionally, governments have been immune from civil suits. Referred to as "sovereign immunity challenges," appellate courts in a number of jurisdictions have now found them responsible for such things as inappropriate parole release, inadequate probation supervision, and failure to arrest a drunk driver who later kills someone.

In drunk driving cases, "dram shop" statutes and case law allow for the drinking establishment that negligently encouraged an intoxicated person to continue drinking, or served a person under the age of twenty-one, to be sued if that person later harms or kills another person.

To pursue any of these sources of financial recovery, you will need to hire a civil attorney. Take the following information into consideration:

> • Shop around. Ask other families in a similar situation who they used and their level of satisfaction. Interview more than one attorney before making a decision. As you interview, ask what kind of cases they handle, how they charge, and what they think about your case. Tell them you will make the decision to retain later.

Remember, however, that the degree of success the attorney has in pursuing a full and fair outcome often depends on investigating the case as soon as possible after the death.

• Look for an attorney who concentrates a significant percentage of his or her practice on personal injury and wrongful death cases. If you use another type of attorney, note when you look at the contract whether additional fees will be required if co-counsel is retained.

• Ask if the attorney has more experience representing plaintiffs or defendants. Ask what percentage of his trials he has won, and what percentage were settled out of court. This will help you analyze how much trial experience the attorney has, which is important. However, the vast majority of lawsuits are settled out of court and do not go to trial.

• Ask for an explanation, in terms you can understand, of the laws in your state that relate to your case, including the statute of limitations. This filing time limit varies by state from six months to six years. Ask for a brief written summary of the merits of the case as the attorney sees it at that point. This will prevent confusion later. Be skeptical, however, of an attorney who promises certain results. Airtight cases simply do not exist.

• Be sure you understand the fee schedule. Does the attorney require a retainer fee to investigate the case? Does the attorney work on a contingency basis (the firm is paid a percentage of the judgment amount)? Does the attorney do any work on an hourly rate basis?

Does the attorney require a promissory note as security for fees? If handling your case on a contingency basis, does the percentage differ if settled out of court, if going to trial, or if going to appeal? Will you be billed for out-of-pocket expenses (court fees, deposition fees) as they occur or will they accumulate and be deducted from the settlement or judgment? If the case is lost, are costs or fees still owed?

• Negotiating fees, carried forth in honest good faith, is professionally acceptable and legal in most states. If state law regulates percentages, the attorney should explain the statute to you.

• If negotiable, you may wish to discuss an hourly fee for work on recovery of actual damages and a contingency rate that decreases as the amount of recovery for punitive damages increases. If there is no significant dispute on liability or damages, and only insurance is recoverable, a contingency fee may be more fair for the hours involved. The attorney may, therefore, work for your insurance recovery on an hourly basis.

• Be sure the employment contract to retain the attorney includes the fee schedule, is complete, specific, and clearly understood before you sign it.

• Ask the attorney for copies of all correspondence relating to your case, and request that he instruct the defendant and/or insurance company to make all offers for settlement in writing.

• Request that bills for services be itemized and match them with the fee agreement.

• Ask for receipts indicating payment and purpose of payment each time you pay your attorney.

If you exercise care in choosing your attorney, you will probably be satisfied with the services. Negligence in civil cases is exceedingly complex and open to a variety of interpretations and strategies. This short discussion can in no way provide information sufficient to understand the intricacies of your particular case. Only your attorney can do that. Sometimes it is impossible for attorneys to give clear and concise opinions about their cases.

If you become dissatisfied, you should discuss your concerns with your attorney. If a satisfactory relationship cannot be achieved, the attorney may be discharged. At the point of discharge, the attorney will be entitled to a fee for services rendered in keeping with the terms of the employment contract.

If you suspect that your attorney's conduct is unethical, you may file a complaint with the local bar association. State Supreme Courts may also disbar, suspend, or censure an attorney for unprofessional conduct. If you wish to take legal action against your attorney, be certain of your facts.

If you win a civil case or settle favorably, plan carefully how you will use the money to avoid excessive taxes. If a large lump sum is received, invest it wisely. You may want to temporarily place it in an interest-bearing account, money market, or other safe but accessible accounts until you can consult with a financial advisor. Eventually, you may want to consider investing in longer term stocks, bonds, and tax-deferred retirement plans or IRAs.

The larger the judgment or settlement, the more likely the offender may offer it as a structured settlement of perhaps a monthly payment over a period of time. While actual damages such as medical costs, funeral expenses, lost wages, and pain and suffering are not taxed, punitive damages are. Since tax implications can be complicated, it would be wise to consult a tax attorney or financial advisor to help you make the best decision.

Bankruptcy

Bankruptcy law has always been complex, but it became even more complex on October 17, 2005, when new bankruptcy laws went into effect. Civil attorneys sometimes tell their clients prematurely that there is no value in filing a civil suit against an offender because, even if found liable, he will probably file bankruptcy to avoid payment. That may or may not be true. It is now harder than it was before to qualify to file bankruptcy. Furthermore, changes have taken place to assure that convicted criminals, including drunk drivers, cannot file personal bankruptcy under Chapters 7 and 13 of the Federal Bankruptcy Code simply to avoid paying civil judgments or to escape paying criminal restitution.

Bars and restaurants sued for irresponsibly serving those already intoxicated or those under the legal drinking age of twenty-one may still file for corporate bankruptcy under Chapter 11.

If your civil attorney suggests that the offender may file bankruptcy, ask him to consult with a qualified bankruptcy attorney. The American Bar Association and most State Bar Associations have bankruptcy sections that can refer you to qualified attorneys.

Crime Victim Compensation

At the beginning of this chapter, it was suggested that families having difficulty with funeral expenses ask their funeral director about the State Crime Victims Compensation Program's funeral benefits for crime victims. All states, the District of Columbia, and the Virgin Islands have Crime Victim Compensation programs that reimburse crime victim families for out-of-pocket non-property expenses. These funds are for victims for which employer benefits, insurance, and civil recovery are not possible. Benefits beyond funeral expenses include medical expenses, lost wages, and other financial needs deemed reasonable. In some states, dependents are eligible for lump sum benefits. All states provide for mental health counseling for injured victims and most pay for counseling for survivors of someone killed.

Since regulations vary from state to state, it is wise to call the victim assistance program of the police department of the prosecutor's office or a local victim group such as Mothers Against Drunk Driving (MADD) or Parents of Murdered Children and request a Crime Victim Compensation application. If you are still unable to learn about the program, call the switchboard of your State Capitol and ask to be connected to the program. Or you can type "(State) Crime Victims Compensation" into your computer browser to learn about the program and download an application.

In all states, the crime must have been reported to the police within three to five days, the victim must not have contributed to the crime, and the victim's family must cooperate with the officials in investigating and prosecuting the case. However, even if the case is not prosecuted, you can still apply for the funds.

You will be expected to submit bills or receipts with the application. Except for emergency awards, applications take weeks or months to process, so application procedures should be initiated as soon as possible. Additional bills may be submitted later. If your claim is denied or you think the award is inadequate, you have the right to appeal.

Costs related directly to the crime can be reimbursed up to the maximum level in each state. These maximums typically range from $10,000 to $25,000, though a few states have higher or lower maximums. If you collect compensation and later collect insurance funds or win a civil suit, you will be required to pay back the compensation to the state.

Restitution

Restitution is money or services ordered by the criminal court to be paid by the offender directly to the victim or surviving family after final conviction. The purpose of restitution is to make the offender personally accountable for his crime and to restore, in part, the victim's loss.

Victim requests for restitution can cover medical and funeral expenses, lost wages, ongoing counseling fees for survivors, or other expenses considered reasonable by the court. Requests for restitution must be accompanied by bills or receipt and should be presented to the Criminal Court judge through the prosecutor or Probation Department before the sentencing hearing. Restitution requests are usually attached to the pre-sentence investigation (PSI) prepared by the Probation Department.

While criminal restitution is a sound concept, it is not a quick or easy solution to financial stress. It is dependent upon the conviction of the offender, which rarely happens until months or years after the crime was committed. Offenders sometimes have limited income from which to pay restitution, especially if they are sent to prison. Procedures for the collection of restitution from the offender and for transferring it to the victim are rarely adequate. Once the offender is out of the criminal justice system (usually meaning completion of probation or parole), a means for monitoring restitution payment no longer exists.

Most states now require that restitution be ordered unless the judge states in the record the reason for not doing so. A few states automatically attach a civil lien to the criminal judgment in order to assure payment after the criminal case is closed. In most cases, unless a substantial lump sum restitution order is ordered immediately following a trial (which will only happen if the offender has the means to pay), chances of actually receiving restitution are slim. The court can revoke probation or parole for failure to pay restitution, but the offender's probation or parole officer must recommend it to the court. If restitution is not paid in full by the time the offender leaves the criminal justice system, the remainder may be converted to a civil judgment in some states.

Government Social Services

Families with limited income and resources that are faced with the death of a loved one, particularly if that loved one was a wage earner, may be eligible for emergency short-term assistance from city or county social services agencies. This assistance may include vouchers for rent, utilities, food, and medicine, but rarely cash. When a wage earner is killed, the surviving parent of dependent children may qualify for Temporary Assistance for Needy Families (TANF), commonly known as welfare. TANF is a monthly cash assistance program for poor families with children under age 18. A family of three (mother and two children) may qualify for TANF if their gross income is below $784 a month and their assets are worth less than $1,000.

There is a four-year lifetime limit on cash assistance. Work is a major component of TANF. Adult recipients with a child over age 1 will be required to participate in a work activity. These work activities help recipients gain the experience needed to find a job and become self-sufficient. Persons who think they may qualify for TANF and its affiliated programs should apply at their local State Department of Human Resources or equivalent agency. It usually takes several weeks to begin receiving a check or food stamps.

A Final but Very Important Reminder

Try to refrain from making unnecessary major financial decisions until a year or more after your loved one's death. Once all the death benefits have been accumulated, it is usually best to leave money where it is unless it becomes crucial to pay bills. Especially beware of unsolicited advice from investment sales people who may contact you. Decisions about significant revisions of your will, moving, investments, or sale of properties, for example, are better considered after your life has settled down a bit and after your capacity for clear and rational thinking has been restored. Don't wait too long, though, to re-draft your will to reflect new beneficiaries.

What I Want to Remember from This Chapter

Chapter Fourteen

CONCLUSION

Each year, about 2 million people receive the shocking news that someone they love has been killed. Car crashes, drownings, falls, suicides, homicides, military deaths, and now, unfortunately, terrorist attacks shatter the lives not only of immediate family members but at least ten other relatives, colleagues, and close friends.

Dying and being killed differ dramatically. Those whose loved ones are killed have no time to psychologically prepare. They are denied the opportunity to say "Goodbye," "I love you," or "I'm sorry." Talk about stages of grief and grief following anticipated deaths simply doesn't work for these survivors. In addition to being thrown into shock at the news, men and women, boys and girls are deeply troubled by the fact that their loved one's body was severely damaged during the process. That hurts profoundly, even though their faith may assure them that their loved one's spirit is now at peace. Killing doesn't just happen; it is someone's fault either by intentional choice or negligence. Difficult to comprehend emotionally, this fact also thrusts surviving family members into the complex and confusing criminal justice system. Many families must negotiate with insurance companies and trial lawyers. They may face financial crises all the way from paying for unplanned funerals to loss of a family breadwinner.

One of the wonders of most human beings is their basic, inherent tendency to recover from the effects of trauma. Yet, recovery is rarely, if ever, complete after a loved one has been senselessly killed.

Sorrow, anger, and frustration with injustice following such a death cause pain that is treatable, but difficult to cure. Time is a significant component. Trauma grief work cannot be "pushed through." It has to be experienced little by little over time.

As a surviving family member or close friend or colleague, you are striving to refocus your sight on life rather than death. You may feel like this pilgrimage is one step forward, then two steps backward. Grief spasms may surprise you with their frequency. Many are astounded at the eruption of grieving when they least expect it.

Resiliency

It is hoped that this book frees you to express your feelings, to choose how and when you will work on feeling better, and to discard, without guilt, the ill advice of those who care but do not understand.

It is hoped that the suggestions offered will help you realize that getting better means talking about what has happened when you want to and with whom you want to. Some people clearly hurt you more than they help. Some don't affect you much one way or the other. A few know how to listen and support, giving advice only when it is asked for. Spend as much time as you can with them.

Getting better means being patient with yourself when progress is slow. It means finding positive things to do. It means realizing that some thread of good can come from the ashes of despair.

Successful care-giving to families enduring a sudden death requires a gentle spirit and a great deal of patience. Helping means being a good listener. It means refraining from judgment. It means avoiding clichés that attempt to talk people out of their feelings. It means reaching out in tangible ways, especially on holidays and anniversaries. It means talking fondly of memories of the deceased loved one. It means assertively guiding victims through the criminal justice process and advocating financially for them, if necessary.

Most significantly, however, it is hoped that, after reading the comments of the many family members and friends in this book, those survivors who have been forced into pain they did not ask for and did not deserve will feel less alone and better understood. Walking in the shoes of a fellow struggler has a healing power all its own. Knowing that someone else understands something of their journey and genuinely cares is a gift to be treasured.

Notes:

RESOURCES

National Organizations That Help Families
When Someone Is Killed

American Association of Suicidology
www.suicidology.org
5221 Wisconsin Avenue NW, Washington, DC 20015
202-237-2280 / 800-273-TALK (8255)
(fax) 202-237-2282

Compassionate Friends
www.compassionatefriends.com
P.O. Box 3696, Oakbrook, IL 60522-3696
630-990-0010 / 877-969-0010 (fax) 630-990-0246

Concerns of Police Survivors (COPS)
www.nationalcops.org
P.O. Box 3199, South Highway Five
Camdenton, MO 65020
573-346-4911   (fax) 573-346-1414

Mothers Against Drunk Driving (MADD)
www.madd.org
511 E. John Carpenter Fwy. #700, Irving, TX 75062
1-877-MADD-HELP   (fax) 972-869-2206

Parents of Murdered Children
www.pomc.com
100 E. 8th Street, B-41, Cincinnati, OH 45202
513-721-5683 / 888-818-POMC   (fax) 513-345-4489

Tragedy Assistance Program for Survivors (TAPS)
(Military Deaths) www.taps.org
1621 Connecticut Avenue NW, Suite 300
Washington, DC 20009
202-588-TAPS (8277) / 800-959-TAPS (8277)

National Organizations That Help All Victims of Crime
Including Families of Those Killed

National Association of Crime Victim
Compensation Boards
www.nacvcb.org
PO Box 7054, Alexandria, VA 22307
703-780-3200   (fax) 703-780-3261

National Center for Victims of Crime
www.ncvc.org
2000 M Street NW, Suite 480, Washington, D.C. 20006
202-467-8700 / 800-FYI-CALL   (fax) 202-467-8701

National Organization for Victim Assistance (NOVA)
www.trynova.org
Courthouse Square
510 King Street, Ste. 424, Alexandria, VA 22314
703-535-6682 / 800-TRY-NOVA (fax) 703-535-5500

National Sheriffs' Association (Victim Program)
www.sheriffs.org
1450 Duke Street, Alexandria, VA 22314
703-836-7827   (fax) 703-683-6541

Office for Victims of Crime (OVC)
www.ovc.gov
U.S. Department of Justice
810 Seventh Street NW, Washington, D.C. 20531
202-307-5983   (fax) 202-305-2446

Office for Victims of Crime Resource Center
www.ojp.usdoj.gov/ovc/ovcres
Box 6000, Rockville, MD 20849-6000
1-800-851-3420

National Trauma and Bereavement Counseling Organizations

American Psychological Association
www.apa.org
750 First Street NE, Washington, D.C. 22002-4242
202-336-5500 / 800-374-2721

Association for Death Education and Counseling
(ADEC) www.adec.org
60 Revere Drive, Suite 500, Northbrook, IL 60062 USA
847-509-0403   (fax) 847-480-9282

Association of Traumatic Stress Specialists
www.atts.info
P.O. Box 246, Phillips, ME 04966
800-991-ATSS (2877)   (fax) 207-639-2434

Center for Loss and Life Transition
www.centerforloss.com
3735 Broken Bow Road, Fort Collins, CO 80526
970-226-6050   (fax) 800-922-6051

International Society for Traumatic Stress Studies
www.istss.org
60 Revere Drive, Suite 500, Northbrook, IL 60062
847-480-9028   (fax) 847-480-9282

National Crime Victims Research and Treatment Center
www.musc.edu/cvc
Medical University of South Carolina
PO Box 250852, Charleston, SC 29425
843-792-2945 (fax) 843-792-3388

National Resources for Civil Suits

National Crime Victim Law Institute
www.ncvli.org
10015 SW Terwilliger Blvd., Portland, OR 97219
503-768-6819   (fax) 503-768-6671

Trial Lawyers for Public Justice, P.C.
www.tlpj.org
1717 Massachusetts Avenue NW, Suite 800
Washington, D.C. 20036
(fax) 202-232-7203

Victim's Assistance Legal Organization (VALOR)
www.valor-national.org
8180 Greensboro Drive, #1070
McLean, VA 22102-3823
703-748-0811   (fax) 703-245-9961

National Medical Resources

American College of Emergency Physicians
www.acep.org
1125 Executive Circle, Irving, TX 75038-2522
972-550-0911 / 800-798-1822
(fax) 972-580-2816

American Trauma Society
www.amtrauma.org
8903 Presidential Parkway, Suite 512
Upper Marlboro, MD 20772
301-420-4189 / 800-556-7890
(fax) 301-420-0617

Brain Injury Association of America
www.biausa.org
8201 Greensboro Dr., Suite 611, McLean, VA 22102
(703)761-0750 / 800-444-6443

Spinal Cord Society
19051 County Hwy 1, Fergus Falls, MN 56537-7609
218-739-5252
(fax) 218-739-5262

National Funeral/Burial Organizations

National Funeral Directors Association
www.nfda.org
13625 Bishop's Drive
Brookfield, WI 53005
262-789-1880 / 800-228-6332
(fax) 262-789-6997

Books and Other Resources

Compassion Books, Inc.
www.compassionbooks.com
7036 State Hwy 80 South, Burnsville, NC 28714
828-675-5909 / 800-970-4220
(fax) 828-675-9687

INDEX

Order Form

No Time For Goodbyes can be ordered by check, money order, Visa, or Mastercard.

Mail or fax this form, or call: **800-970-4220** to place your order.
For orders outside the U.S. call: 828-675-5909
You can also order on our secure website, www.compassionbooks.com

1-9 copies: $12.95 each • 10-19 copies: $9.72 each (25% discount)
20 or more copies: $7.77 each (40% discount)

Shipping:
1 copy: $3.50 • 2 - 9 copies: add $.50 additional postage for each copy.
10 copies or more, add 5% of total

_____copies of *No Time For Goodbyes*, $ _____

Tax (NC only) 7% _____

Shipping_____

Total _____

❑ Enclosed is my check or money order for $_____
Make checks payable to: Compassion Books, Inc.

❑ Please charge my credit card (Visa or MC only)

Card # _____ Exp. date _____

V#_____ (last 3 digits on back of card at end of signature strip)

Ship To:

Name: _____

Organization:_____

Address: _____

City/State/ Zip: _____

Phone _____Fax_____

Mail or Fax your order to: Compassion Books, Inc.
7036 State Hwy. 80 South Burnsville, NC 28714
1-800-970-4220 / (828-675-5909) or Fax: 828-675-9687
email: heal2grow@aol.com • www.compassionbooks.com

For hundreds of carefully chosen resources to help with
grief and loss, comfort, hope, and healing
visit our website at
www.compassionbooks.com